Breaking the Ice

Did you know we have an ambiance Spotify playlist for this book?

Scan this code with your Spotify App:

Our books are also available in e-book.

Find our catalog on:
https://cherry-publishing.com/en/

CHRISTINE TROY

BREAKING THE ICE

© Christine Troy, 2023

© Cherry Publishing, 2024

ISBN: 978-1-80116-784-0

For my Angel, Jasmin.

Introduction

In the heart of our new season, chaos reigns supreme.

It's a siren call that threatens to shatter the unity of my team, just when we're on the brink of the playoffs.

I can't let this happen!

But there's a complication, a name: Emma.

She's my own personal chaos, a temptation too perfect to resist.

With every passing moment, I teeter on the precipice of surrendering to her, risking it all in the process …

1

EMMA

The sound of his ringing cellphone draws my father's attention away from the crowd as we make our way towards the dressing room. Walking beside me is Bill Thornton, my father's old college friend and the coach of the Portland Devils hockey team.

"Max?" Bill Thornton stops beside me, and I follow. My father holds up a hand, asking the caller for a moment, then presses the smartphone to his chest. "I'm sorry, but I have to take this. Go ahead, I'll catch up." With that, he turns away and puts the phone back to his ear.

Thornton nods and signals for me to follow him. He's a tall man with heather gray hair, leading me through a crowded hallway that smells of hot dogs and caramel popcorn. The stadium is alive with excitement, some fans still buzzing from the game. Admittedly, I was thoroughly entertained – the home team, the Devils, methodically outplayed the visitors, the Cougars. Despite my limited knowledge of ice hockey, the drums and cheers of the fan club got me into the spirit, especially after the first period.

"It's remarkable how many women are here," I comment

Breaking the Ice

as the trainer guides me down a flight of stairs to the lower section of the ice rink. I never expected so many young girls to be interested in this sport, and not just any girls – they're all dressed up and stunning. I can't help but feel a bit out of place in my skinny jeans, gray coat, and short boots.

"Yes, we have a growing number of female fans," Thornton replies with a grin. "Can't blame them, though. Our team is the youngest and most attractive in the club's history. Two of our players even made it to the cover of a magazine last month. That's what the ladies are drawn to."

I can imagine that.

"I'm just glad you and your father could step in at such short notice. After Patrick, our previous sports masseur, broke his arm while drunk, I was at my wit's end. Why did that idiot have to party with the players? Everyone knows they're a force to reckon with." Thornton shakes his head and takes a turn. "If I could offer you some advice, never try to keep up with the boys when it comes to drinking. They'll outmatch you without a doubt. Here we are." He stops before a tall door from behind which I can hear voices. "Let's introduce you then." With a proud smile and a wink, Bill gestures for me to enter. You'd think he was leading me into a treasure trove rather than a hockey team's locker room.

A cloud of steam, carrying the scent of shower gel, greets us as he opens the door, revealing a white-tiled room. My eyes are drawn to the massive blood-red team logo emblazoned on the center of the floor – a grinning devil with crossed hockey sticks, reminiscent of a pirate flag. Lockers line the walls on either side, and in front of each stand two long benches, occupied by about twenty men. Most of them are half-dressed, wearing only the towels around their waists.

"Oh my, who do we have here?" One of the guys notices us. He's seated on the bench to my left, wearing nothing but snug white boxer shorts. Through the fabric, his... assets are quite visible. *Not bad. The question is whether he knows how to use it.* I meet his gaze, and he grins back. Surprisingly handsome, he has dark brown eyes and slightly wavy, gelled-back hair. I believe they call this hairstyle 'the flow' – quite popular among hockey players. My eyes trail down his heavily tattooed torso. While I don't appreciate every design, like the faded rose on his collarbone, I do admire his passion for body art. I have a few tattoos of my own. His grin widens as he catches me scanning him – the guy is clearly a Player.

"Wow, Coach, did you bring that beauty just for me? That's thoughtful, but unnecessary," the guy next to him chimes in, raising his eyebrows playfully. Towering over his teammate, he's lean with dark cropped hair, and his eyes are the bluest I've seen. Only one tattoo graces his skin – a sun covering part of his chest. He whistles appreciatively. By now, we certainly have the attention of everyone present.

"Oh, wow, sweetheart, I might be finished, but I wouldn't mind another shower with you," a big red-haired guy interjects, unfastening his jeans' belt provocatively.

"Hold on, Toby, I saw her first," the sun-tattooed guy remarks, inciting a chorus of loud shouts from the other players.

"Forget it, she needs a real man!"

"Hey, gorgeous, want me to show you my moves?"

"Hey, sexy, bet on me – you won't lose!"

"Quiet!" Thornton's voice suddenly thunders beside me. There's something amusing about this little man silencing a group of giants. "Settle down," he scolds, his gaze sweeping across the athletes. "Let me introduce you. This is Emmina Tade Hoang. She'll be taking over for Patrick for the rest of the season."

"Emma is fine," I interject. I hate my full name – Emmina sounds excessively old-fashioned, and three quarters of people mispronounce Hoang.

"What? Little missy is our masseuse?" Toby's eyes widen.

"Well, that's perfect. She can start with me right away." With those words, he turns, presenting his back and pulling up his shirt slightly. His jeans also slip down a bit, revealing his hairy rear.

"Come on, Toby, put your 'butt mullet' away," the sun-tattooed guy exclaims, catching sight of his teammate's exposed backside. Grabbing a nearby towel, he playfully whips Toby's bare skin.

"Dude, Parker, knock it off!" Toby retaliates, attempting to put Parker in a headlock. Bill Thornton intervenes, calling for silence.

"That's enough! Neither of you will be getting a massage from Emma."

"What?" the two protest simultaneously.

"Then who's going to take care of us?" Parker inquires.

"Her father, Maxwell."

"I don't get it. Are we having two massage therapists now?" Toby furrows his brows and pulls up his pants.

"Exactly, genius." Hands on his hips, Thornton marches through the rows of benches like a sergeant. "After you drove away Mrs. Limes, your previous masseuse..."

"Wait, what? The old hag scared us off! Have you seen her hands?" Parker interrupts the coach, shaking his head in disgust. "Even my grandma doesn't have fingers that gnarled."

Ignoring his player's distaste, Bill continues, "After you offended Mrs. Limes, scared off Ms. Waterbay with your jokes, and upset her replacement, Thomas, I thought you didn't deserve a new masseuse."

"That's not fair, Thomas had it coming! Have you smelled his breath?" Parker interjects, and Bill turns his attention to him.

Breaking the Ice

"Will you let me finish? Or do you want to do extra laps around the rink first?"

"Okay, okay, I'm good." Parker raises his hands apologetically. "I'm just telling it how it is."

"Anyway, if it were up to me, you wouldn't have a new massage therapist. But the board of directors had a different opinion and arranged for Maxwell." The coach's gaze shifts to the player, who's sitting there with a wide grin.

"What? Don't look at me like that. It's not my fault Pat tripped and broke his arm."

"No, Durand," Thornton growls, "you're the one who got him drunk."

"So what? How was I supposed to know he couldn't handle his liquor?" Before he continues, the player turns his attention to me, locking eyes. "Sorry, Coach, but only those who can keep up should play with the big boys." His expression as he says this is unmistakable. Durand, the guy with the upper body tattoo, is hitting on me.

Obviously, he believes his charms or that sultry gaze will work on me. I admit, he's handsome and he seems to have a reputation with the ladies. However, I'm not particularly drawn to show-offs. But for the fun of it, I decide to play along. I give him a meaningful smile and bite my lower lip. A triumphant grin spreads across his face. Let's see how he handles a little competition, I think, shifting my gaze to Parker, his bench mate. I offer him a brief, innocent smile, and his features brighten, freezing Durand's grin. Out of the corner of my eye, I catch Durand's bewildered glance towards Parker. I barely suppress a smile.

"Durand's right. If Pat can't handle it, he shouldn't be celebrating with us," another player joins the conversation, diverting my attention back to the coach.

"I couldn't care less about your drinking prowess," Thornton retorts. "I have better things to do than find new masseurs every two weeks. Let me make one thing clear: Emma here..." Bill steps closer to me, placing his hands on my shoulders. "... Is your last chance. If you dare to alienate her or her father, I'll personally ensure that they're your last enjoyable massage therapists. Then I'll find some burly, unpolished men to knead you like dough." As Thornton explains, a mental image forms – a flat-nosed giant with lifeless eyes and a blunt demeanor, bending the players in all directions during massages. Judging by the expressions on the athletes' faces, similar thoughts cross their minds. Only Durand remains unfazed, looking at me with an inscrutable expression before turning back to the coach. "Don't worry, Coach, we'll behave. Right, guys?" His words sound sincere, but Durand's gaze tells a different story. He looks like he's plotting something. Amidst the mumbling agreement of his teammates, I wonder what his game is.

"Look..." Durand stands up and raises his palms. "... Emma and her father are in good company with us." Before Thornton can respond, there's a knock on the door. My dad enters and apologizes for arriving late. All eyes turn to him, all except Durand's and mine. The player keeps his dark eyes locked onto me. I see him lick his lips seductively as I meet his gaze boldly. He's not the tallest, maybe five-foot-five, but he's undeniably well-built. And he knows it. Confidence oozes from him. *Well*, I think to myself, *there's likely nothing serious here, but a little flirtation might be on the table.* I glance over the other men, most of whom are also quite attractive. *Yes, I believe I'm going to enjoy this new job.*

2

CALEB

Feeling deeply satisfied with our team's performance, I turn off the shower and step out of the locker room. As usual, I'm the last one to finish. But that's fine by me; it gives me some peace and quiet. Especially after crucial games, like today, I always need some time to unwind. And since hot water is the only thing that helps me relieve stress, I often spend twenty minutes or more under the shower.

With the unbelieving face of the Cougars' captain in my mind, I take a few steps to the opposite wall. *He and his guys won't be sitting comfortably for weeks after the thrashing we've given them.* Satisfied, I grab one of the towels from the shelves and start drying off. We sent them home with a seven-to-one defeat. Another team that underestimated us underdogs. If this keeps up, we're going to make it to the playoffs. And there, I've promised myself, I won't give a hundred percent, but a thousand. By the end of the season, the name Caleb Whyler will represent professional hockey. I'll be the Tiger Woods of the ice.

With the towel draped around my neck, I walk through the short corridor leading to the locker room. My teammates are

Breaking the Ice

sitting quietly, which is unusual, all looking towards the exit where I just saw the coach disappear.

"What's going on here? Did I miss something?" I ask, toweling off the back of my head.

"You could say that," my best buddy Parker explains, turning around with a goofy grin. "We got a new masseuse."

"And?" I shrug and walk to my locker.

"And she's a damn bombshell! I'm telling you, I'm gonna score with that girl."

"Don't make a fool of yourself, Parker," Durand chimes in, turning to face my friend who's sitting on the bench behind him. "That girl is out of your league; she needs a real man."

Physically, he's outmatched by the heavily tattooed Canadian. He doesn't have nearly as broad a chest or powerful legs. And compared to Durand's muscular arms, his look like spaghetti. However, Parker is a whole head taller.

"Well, buddy, hate to disappoint you. Maybe you're a big shot in Canada, but here in America, women need real guys, not garden gnomes."

"Oh, you mean grasshoppers like you who weigh less than the woman herself? Well, that's something I definitely can't provide."

"Alright, guys, cut it out," I mutter as I step into my jeans. I skip the boxer shorts, after all, I've got plans for today.

"No, Caleb, I won't cut it out. Our womanizer here really thinks he's better." God dammit, this is starting again. The eternal power struggle between Parker and Durand. And who's responsible for that? None other than Thornton. At the beginning of the season, he gave both of them the assistant title. He knows exactly what show-offs they are. This has only spurred them on more to outdo each other. While it might occasionally help on the ice, it's simply annoying in daily life because they're always at each other's throats. I advised Thornton to assign the

Breaking the Ice

assistant title to two other players, but the stubborn old mule wouldn't listen. He seems unconcerned that he's playing with a ticking time bomb that's bound to explode sooner or later. I swear, that one day, they'll be at each other's throats and out of commission for the rest of the season.

"I don't know if you've got anything between your ears, Parker, but the way the sweetheart was staring, it was clear," Durand adds.

"Yeah, clearly she's interested in me."

"Don't make me laugh!" Durand lets out a feigned chuckle. The tension in the air is dangerously palpable, something the others notice too. All eyes are on the two arguing men.

"Cut it out, or I'll wipe that grin off your face," Parker growls, clenching his fists.

"Alright, now calm down, okay?" I raise my hands in a soothing gesture as I approach the two. "We're on the brink of entering the playoffs. We've got a crucial game coming up next Sunday. We really should be focusing on the championship."

"Feel free, Beanpole," Durand bypasses my attempt at mediation, takes a step toward Parker, and looks up at him with a venomous glare. *Oh damn, does it have to be like this?*

"Come on, let's drop it, you two," I attempt one last time.

"Yeah," Toby chimes in, moving towards them and placing his gigantic hands on each of their shoulders. "No need for fisticuffs. How about you make a bet instead?" I squint. This is the lousiest idea he could have come up with, and at the same time, so typical of him. I don't know if all Swiss people are like this, resolving every issue with some kind of bet. Toby definitely gets a kick out of it.

"And what do you have in mind?" Durand sounds skeptical but not uninterested.

"Well, you could bet on who can bed the girl first. Let's say you have until the finals."

"Finals? We're not even sure to get that far yet."

"I'm firmly convinced that we can make it. What do you guys think, are you with me?" A unanimous roar of agreement ripples through the locker room. Each of us is laser-focused on winning the championship. And honestly, from where I stand, we've got a real shot at it.

"Even if we don't make it that far, I'd say we agree on the finals as the cutoff. Alright with you?" Toby's gaze shifts from Parker to Durand.

"Fine by me," he says. "But if I win, Parker shaves his eyebrows and his flow."

Durand raises his hand to his head, running his fingers through his brown hair. The crease that forms between his brows reveals his uncertainty.

"What? Losing your nerve?" Parker provokes him, crossing his arms over his chest. "Afraid of losing?"

"Against a wimp like you? Definitely not. I'm in."

"And if neither of you manages to get the girl?" I ask. I know Toby and his crazy bets; I'm sure there's more to come.

"Unlikely. You'll see; by the end of the month, my fingers will smell like that girl's lady juice." Durand's grin is smug.

"In case Emma throws both of them off the bed, they either fulfill their respective bet conditions or wash our jockstraps for a week," the Swiss guy explains with a diabolical glint in his eye. Suppressing a gag at the thought of sweaty cup protectors, I see some of us aren't exactly hygiene conscious. I don't even want to imagine what else might be clinging to them aside from sweat and ball hair. Parker seems to share the sentiment, as I can see him visibly shudder in disgust.

"I am in favor of redeeming the personal bet stakes." He declares.

"Works for me," Durand shrugs unimpressed. "I'm going to win, anyway."

Breaking the Ice

"Dream on, Canadian. Emma will pick me. No woman wants a towering meter stick like you."

"Oh yeah, you..."

"Hold on, hold on, hold on!" Toby steps between the two, giving them a 'shut up already' look. "So, just to spell it out for the slow ones: You've got until the finals to bed, Emma. If Parker gets there first and scores with her, Durand gets his head shaved along with his eyebrows. If Durand wins the bet, he gets three free shots on a naked Parker."

"With a cup and a helmet," my rather pale friend adds.

"With a cup and a helmet, of course," Toby rolls his eyes. "And in case neither of you big mouths manages to bed Emma, you both have to fulfill your respective bets."

While the Swiss guy lays down the rules again, Parker and Durand lock eyes with hatred.

"So, gentlemen, do we have a deal?" Toby looks between the two with eyebrows raised in expectation.

"Deal," Parker grumbles.

"Deal," Durand confirms.

"Excellent!" Toby cheers as the two shake hands to seal their pact. "In that case, as the designated bet commissioner, there's only one thing left for me to say: Let the games begin!" Another round of cheering echoes through the locker room, and some of the players cheer on their favorites. Great, now the whole team is focused on this stupid bet instead of our goal. Heaven help us if this crap affects our performance. Then I'll rip Toby a new one and give that damn Emma a piece of my mind too. Whatever kind of girl she is, one thing's for sure: She's already getting on my nerves.

3

EMMA

"Come in. Mr. Flake should be here any moment now," Bill leads my father and me into an elegantly furnished office. The floor is made of dark marble, and expensive-looking paintings hang on the walls. Towards the back, in front of a floor-to-ceiling window, is a massive desk. I believe it's made of mahogany. In any case, it's polished to a high shine and practically screams wealth. Thornton's phone rings and we turn towards him. "That's the General Manager; he's calling about a player transfer. Please take a seat; the boss will be here shortly," he explains, gesturing towards two chairs in front of the desk. As we follow his instructions, he exits the room.

"So, what do you think?" Dad asks as soon as we're seated. His hazel eyes are fixed on me.

"About what?"

"Well, about all of this." He smiles and draws circles with an elevated index finger. "I know I sprung the job on you. But it's a great opportunity, trust me."

And it really is. Originally, I had planned to start working at my father's practice after completing my massage therapy training. He's been a self-employed therapeutic masseur

Breaking the Ice

with various additional certifications for many years – including sports massage. In our hometown of Aberdeen, he's a renowned expert. Typically, his schedule is booked months in advance, and he doesn't take on new patients. So, it surprised me even more when he suddenly closed his practice to work for the Portland Devils. Fresh out of university, he brought me along in his paternal care. While that's incredibly kind of him, it's also quite stressful for me. I mean, this job is throwing me into the deep end.

"What if I make mistakes?" I voice my biggest concern. "The Devils are professionals; imagine if I use the wrong technique and pull a muscle on one of them."

"You won't, Emma." Dad places his hand on my knee and gives it a gentle squeeze. "Stop doubting yourself, okay? You're an excellent masseuse, and you'll excel at this job."

"Let's hope you're right, and that the players and him here see it the same way." I nod my head towards the opposite side of the desk. It strikes me that there's neither a chair nor an executive chair over there. Odd.

"If you encounter any unexpected problems, come to me," he insists. "But you'll see, you'll handle all of this effortlessly." Now, before I can respond, the door behind us opens.

"Ah, excellent, you're already here," a husky voice sounds. We turn towards it and discover a dark-blond man in his mid-forties. He sits in an electric wheelchair and rolls straight towards us. "Glad you could arrange to come so spontaneously," he remarks, stopping in front of my father. My father stands up and extends his hand. "Mr. Flake, pleased to meet you."

"Oh, the pleasure is all mine, Mr. Tade. I've heard quite a bit about your magical hands. One could say your reputation precedes you. And you must be the daughter, Emmina."

"Emma is fine, and yes, I'm his daughter. Nice to meet you," I reply, shaking our new boss's hand and studying his

Breaking the Ice

appearance a bit more closely. He's slender, wearing a designer suit, and polished shoes. His eyes are a deep-sea blue, and his nose is straight. Overall, he would be a dapper man if not for that nasty scar on his face. It's about as thick as a finger, resembling a burst sausage, running across the lower right side of his face. It has left behind a swollen pink area where it crosses his lips. I have to resist staring at the disfigured spot.

"Well, I assume Coach Thornton has already introduced you to the guys," Mr. Flake inquires as he rolls his wheelchair behind the desk to his seat.

"Yes, Bill has already introduced us. You have a great team," my father answers, visibly swelling the owner's chest.

"To be honest, the team is my pride and joy. You know, my wife thinks the Devils are a pure waste of time and money. And yes, I admit, the team doesn't bring in nearly as much as my other projects." From Dad, I know that Flake is involved in European real estate trading and is quite wealthy. "But it's not about money for me. This team is more of a hobby, a passion, if you will." Flake's lips curl into a sincere smile. "I want the guys to achieve what I couldn't after my car accident."

"You played hockey yourself," I deduce, seeing a painful expression flit across his features. His reaction is swift, like a flutter of wings, but I don't miss it.

"Yes, for many years. I was a forward for the Milwaukee Rangers. In my last year on the ice, we had just made it to the playoffs when the accident happened." He rests his forearms on the table and laces his fingers together. "That was over twenty years ago. I've grown accustomed to my new life and made the best of it. I found a new challenge in real estate, and as it turned out, I had a knack for it. You're probably wondering why I'm telling you all of this. Well, as you've noticed, even after all these years, my heart still beats for ice hockey. Missing out on the playoffs back then still weighs on me. It's

Breaking the Ice

like something is missing from my life. Something that can't be bought with any amount of money in the world." Even though Mr. Flake doesn't show it, I'm certain that opening up about this issue affects him. "Anyway, I'm very invested in seeing my Devils win the championship. When it comes to the team, I spare no expense or effort. The guys should have everything they need to succeed. And that's where you both come in." Flake looks at my father and then at me intently. "I expect your full commitment. All team members, if they wish, will receive pre-training and post-game massages. It's essential to avoid strains or muscle tears. Moreover, I expect you to be available at all times, day or night, until the end of the season. The guys should be able to call on your magical hands anytime. Naturally, I'll compensate you accordingly for your efforts. In addition to your agreed-upon fee, I'll pay you a bonus of eight hundred dollars for each round the guys make it through unharmed." Wow! Eight hundred dollars as a bonus – and that's per won game? I feel my mouth drop open and quickly close it again. Dad beside me seems less surprised by the information. He appears unfazed and merely nods. "You see," Flake continues, "I truly care about the Devils and the championship. So, please do me the favor and give it your best." While the owner and my father discuss a few more trivial matters, I ponder what I could do with all that money. There are six games left until the playoffs. The playoffs themselves have seven rounds, then comes the semifinals... Even if they only make it that far, that's thirteen games, if I'm keeping it straight in my head, which means $10,400. Insane!

After the conversation with Flake, he sends us down to the basement, where Thornton is waiting for us. Now that the corridors are no longer swarmed with visitors, he gives us a tour. We're shown everything from the souvenir shop to the stands, the VIP area, the commentator's booth, the gym, and the ice rink. Lastly, Bill leads us to our new workplace – two comfortably furnished massage rooms with adjoining bathrooms. They're right next to each other. My father's room is slightly larger than mine and features a desk. Otherwise, the rooms are identical. Both have a massage table, a sideboard filled with towels, a shelf with massage oils, and some greenery in the form of dragon trees. The ceiling lights are dimmable, and the floor is made of parquet, giving the room a pleasant warmth.

"In case you work with aromatherapy, we're well equipped in that area," the coach explains, placing a hand on a top shelf. Numerous brown glass bottles stand there. "Our first massage therapist insisted on relaxation music. If you want something like that, just let us know. In fact, if there's anything you need, just tell us."

"Well, for my part, I could really use a proper coffee right now," my father remarks. "Emma and I have been on our feet for fourteen hours."

"Right, I completely forgot. You two just arrived today. Alright then, let's go upstairs and get you some coffee and something to eat. After that, I'll show you your apartment."

"That sounds like a fantastic idea," Dad says, walking alongside Bill towards the door. "Emma?" He turns to me when he realizes I'm not following them. "Are you coming?"

"Yeah, in a bit. I just want to take a look around."

"I can understand that. Come on, Max, let your daughter have some time to explore everything." With that, Bill pats my old man on the shoulder and winks at me. "Alright then, we'll wait for you upstairs."

"Got it." While the two of them disappear through the open door into the hallway, I survey my new workplace. I run my fingertips over the shelves and the sideboard, gaze at the landscape paintings on the walls. Unbelievable, they're actually giving me, a newcomer, my own treatment room. I wouldn't

Breaking the Ice

have dreamed of it. I had actually thought I'd be more like an assistant, just helping out my father. I never would have dared to dream that I'd be seen as a full-fledged massage therapist. Honestly, I couldn't have found a better job. Even Dad's practice pales in comparison to this. My chest tightens with excitement. Although I still feel a sense of admiration for it all, I can't wait to get started.

Smiling with anticipation, I stand at the head of the massage table and admire it. The thing looks brand-new and incredibly expensive. It's covered in buttons and levers for adjusting height and who knows what else.

"I figured I'd find you here," a male voice startles me. I glance towards the door and see the guy with the sun tattoo leaning against the doorframe.

"Oh, hey, I didn't even hear you come in. Parker, right?"

"Ethan Parker," he confirms, entering and extending his hand towards me. "But you can just call me Parker; that's what everyone does around here." The look he gives me as I shake his hand is captivating. His eyes are a unique ice blue, as I can see up close. I feel like I'm drowning in them if I look long enough. The dark lashes enhance the effect. Back when I was a young girl, I would have mentioned his sensational eyes. I probably would have misinterpreted his gaze and thought he was just being friendly. Today, I know how men work, and I'm aware that he's here because he's interested in me. I find that sweet, he's sweet. Even though he's not exactly my type. But he's perfect for a little flirting and to make the time more enjoyable.

"Pleased to meet you," I say, pulling my hand back while letting my thumb lightly brush against the back of his hand. The touch is delicate and appears accidental. And for that reason, I'm aware, it has its full effect.

"Yeah, um... I'm pleased as well," he says, lowering his gaze to his hand and rubbing the spot where my thumb brushed against him.

"So, Parker," I say, tilting my head slightly to the side, "have you been playing for the Devils for long?"

"I, uh... this is my second year." Parker removes his gaze from my thighs and looks at me. "Mr. Flake hired me last year when he bought the team."

"So, you've played here from the very beginning?"

"You could say that, yes."

"And what can I do for you?" I ask, leaning against the massage table in a sensual motion, crossing my legs. "Are you looking for a massage?"

"I'm actually here to see if I can do something for you," he answers. I believe this statement has a double meaning. But Parker isn't a Player, which is why the words sound like he's just checking on me. Making sure everything's okay with the newcomer.

"That's kind of you, but I have everything I need. Thanks." With a little hop, I stand up from the massage table. I take a couple of steps towards him and glance up at him through my lashes. "Is there anything else?"

He hesitates, as if carefully considering his words.

"No, as I said, I just wanted to see if I could assist you." Another suggestive innuendo? Well, if this is his way of flirting, then the guy is pretty unsubtle.

"Okay, then I should get going," I reply, not addressing his comment, and walk past him towards the door. I hear him curse behind me. *Well, my friend*, I think, *you're cursing rightly because you've just messed things up.* I love to flirt, but when men become pushy or, like in his case, blunt, the whole thing loses its charm. Hand on the light switch, I look at him expectantly. He catches on, shoves his hands in his pockets, and steps out of the massage room in front of me.

Breaking the Ice

"Well, then," I say, after turning off the light and closing the door behind us, "I'll see you tomorrow." With that, I leave him standing and head upstairs to Dad and Bill. It's high time for a decent coffee and a nice sandwich.

4

CALEB

Arching her back, Jess presents her round butt to me as I press against her. "Oh God, Caleb! Damn, yes!" she moans beneath me.

"Hush, Jess, not so loud," I attempt to stifle her increasingly throaty moans of ecstasy. In vain, she's on the verge of orgasm and can't control herself any longer. Trying to avoid broadcasting our intercourse throughout the entire house, I hasten to bring things to a conclusion. Continuing my forceful thrusts, I also deliver a slap to her butt. I'm well aware of how much she enjoys it, and indeed, I coax a satisfying grunt of pleasure from her. I repeat the spanking, this time on the opposite cheek, pushing her over the edge. "Fuck, Caleb! Yes, yes, YES!" Her fingers claw into the sheets as shudders of pleasure run through her and she climaxes. I can feel her juices running down my balls. Though I'd love to keep on fucking, I'm assuming that someone might have heard us. So, a knock on her door could be imminent. I place my hands on her hips, pulling her closer to me, and seek my own release. Just before reaching that point, I pull my cock out of Jessica and ejaculate onto her backside. I love watching myself come on her back.

And given her willingness, I wholeheartedly indulge in this fetish. Tilting my head back, I close my eyes. A single raw gasp escapes my lips, just before the expected knock on the door.

"Yes?" Jess calls out, still breathless.

"Darling, Anna has prepared dinner, we're eating now!" That's Veronica, Jessica's mom. Her words sound neutral, but a trace of disgust is evident in her voice. She can't stand me and believes I'm too old for her 19-year-old daughter. Maybe she's right; after all, I'm 27, a whole eight years older than her precious sunshine.

"Alright, we'll be there in a minute!" my girlfriend calls toward the bedroom door. Then she brushes her blonde hair behind her ear and shoots me a seductive glance over her shoulder. "So, Mister, I'd say that was damn hot!"

"One could say that," I reply with a grin, reaching for the tissue box on her nightstand to clean up. Usually, we take a shower together after sex, but that's not possible today since her parents are waiting for dinner. I hate being here; I feel more comfortable in my own apartment. There, we can be as loud as we want and walk around naked all day long. Much to my annoyance, Jess insists that we spend a night at her place once a week. Like tonight.

As I swiftly put on my clothes, she takes her time.

"Come on, Jess, you know they're waiting," I urge, leading the way to the door.

"Man, relax, Caleb. They're not going to break a sweat if they have to wait a few minutes," she replies, indifferent to her mother's opinion of me. No, even worse, she finds amusement in her narrow-minded thinking and delights in provoking her. Hand on the doorknob, I look back at her. Jess is still sitting naked on the bed, slowly putting on her bra. It's annoying.

"Could you hurry up a bit?" I ask.

"Could you be a bit more polite?" she retorts. "I'm coming,

okay?"

Fifteen damned minutes later, we finally make it and enter the dining room of the Flake family, furnished with designer furniture and chandeliers. Like everything else in the house, this room oozes wealth and elegance.

"Caleb, my boy, so nice to see you," greets me Carl Flake, owner of the Portland Devils. He's sitting in his wheelchair at the head of the table, set with silverware and crystal glasses, smiling benevolently at us. Even though he always treats me kindly, I feel foolish sitting next to him and pretending like nothing happened. I mean, just a few minutes ago, I was banging his daughter, and now I'm here, supposed to have dinner with him and his family.

"Take a seat next to me, lad," he insists, motioning to the spot beside him. I oblige, and Jess sits down as well. She's focused on her mother, who has pursed her lips into a thin line. From the corner of my eye, I see Jessica smirking challengingly at her. Their relationship is strained. Jess claims her mother is a selfish bitch who only married her dad for his money. Money she passionately spends daily. According to Jess, Veronika never loved her husband and made no secret of it. But she seems to care a lot about her daughter. Her only child. As far as she's concerned, her girl should snag a rich businessman so she can be well taken care of and live a carefree life. A hockey player like me, even if I play in the pro league, is beneath her daughter's level. After all, a sports career isn't permanent. The best example of that is her own husband, Carl. A minor accident, and that was it for his career. Even if you stay in good health, you eventually become too old for the pros. And then the big money is gone too.

"You were brilliant today, my boy," Mr. Flake redirects my attention. "The Cougars are one of the strongest teams, but you really put them in their place." Jess slides her hand under

Breaking the Ice

the table onto my thigh and squeezes it, all the while beaming at her dad. She's incredibly proud of me and my performance.

"We all put them in their place - the whole team. The guys were great today," I correct him. But the owner shakes his head, leans in slightly toward me, and looks at me intently.

"You were great, Caleb. No false modesty, you're the star of the team - the driving force, if you will. Without you, the guys are nothing." That's not true. Every single one of us is exceptional in their own way and damn good on the ice. But I suppose Carl is comparing me to himself. He sees his younger self in me. The version of him that got injured just before the playoffs thanks to that car accident. "You know what, let's drink to that. Anna!" He beckons to the housekeeper, who's just bringing in a roast. The lady is around sixty, with gray hair tied in a bun, and she's my favorite person in the house after Jess. Anna reminds me of my mom - even though she's ten years younger. The soft facial features, the gentle demeanor, and the melodious voice. Yes, she's like my mother.

"Yes, Sir?"

"Bring Caleb and me a whiskey."

"Carl!" Veronika protests, her lips still tightly pursed. "You know very well you're not supposed to drink. Dr. Glenfield forbids it because of the medication."

"Oh, good old Glenfield should relax, it's just a glass."

"You're beyond redemption."

"I know." Flake shrugs and turns to Anna again. "Bring us two glasses. Chilled."

"Yes, Sir."

"And Anna, take the thirty-year-old bottle, you know, the good stuff." The housekeeper nods and leaves. "So, Caleb, a seven-to-one victory. Six of those goals were your doing. If that's not an impressive performance, I don't know what is." I contemplate reminding him that five of those goals were thanks

Breaking the Ice

to Parker's perfect pass, but I refrain. Carl would downplay my buddy's contribution. To him, only what I, his 'star', achieved matters. That does have its benefits on one side - I'm paid better and enjoy luxuries that my teammates don't get - but it also has downsides like pressure to perform and players resenting my special treatment. It creates chaos within the team.

"Today's game went pretty well," I say, as he waits for my response.

"Well? It was amazing!" He energetically slams his fist on the table. Before he can launch into more praise, Anna appears and brings our drinks. "So, here's to you, Caleb. And to the championship."

"To the championship," I say, and my boss clinks glasses with me so enthusiastically that the ice cubes in our glasses tinkle.

"Oh, one more thing..." Carl takes a sip and sets the whiskey aside. "As you know, we've got two new massage therapists. Maxwell Tade and his daughter Emma."

"What?" Jess interjects into our conversation. "Another woman? I thought the team was only getting men from now on, because they're easier to deal with and tougher."

"That was the original plan, my dear. But Bill changed his mind. Why do you ask? Does it bother you?"

"What? No, I couldn't care less! But she's going to be a poor thing surrounded by all those testosterone-laden apes. Let's hope the players don't drive her away like they did with the previous female masseuses." I shift my gaze to my girlfriend, seeing a muscle twitch on her cheek. She's not concerned for a second about the masseuse or the players misbehaving. No, Jess simply doesn't like the idea of another woman touching me.

"Anyway, Caleb, I wish for you to avail yourself of their services, daily. The same goes for Parker and Durand. But I've already discussed that with them." Carl's statement elicits a snort from my girlfriend. I quickly put my hand on her thigh to calm her down, though it doesn't work.

"Dad, daily treatments are totally excessive," she hisses.

"No, not at all." Flake looks at his daughter with a stern expression. "We're on the verge of the playoffs, and Caleb is our top player. We can't risk strains or muscle tears, so I insist on the massages. You'll have to come to terms with it." That was clear. Carl won't tolerate any objections, as Jess understands. With a face flushed in anger, she glares at her old man. She's used to getting what she wants. But in this case, her father remains firm. He ignores her irritation and turns back to me. "I don't care whether you get the massage before or after practice. Do what suits you."

"But I'm in top shape, I'm fine," I counter.

"And it needs to stay that way. That's why I demand you get daily treatment." I can already see he won't negotiate on this matter. So, I nod, even if it means I'll have a moody girlfriend for the foreseeable future. For the second time today, I'm annoyed by our new masseuse.

"Can we finally start eating, or do you plan on discussing your hobby even longer?" Veronika snarks from the other end of the table, looking at her husband in exasperation. Her face is stony, lines of tension between her eyebrows and around her mouth. She could be a beautiful woman if she weren't so perpetually disgruntled. Like Jessica, she has delicate features, a small nose, and full, natural blond hair. Her slender figure and small breasts also resemble her daughter's. Only Jess inherited her blue eyes from her dad.

"Alright, alright," Carl concedes, giving the cranky woman a sympathetic smile. "Enough talk about the team."

Dinner is like every meal at the Flake house. Exhausting. Veronika poisons the atmosphere with her foul mood, which

Breaking the Ice

everyone else ignores. The roast is fantastic, the cornbread, the sauces, and the vegetables are delicious. Nevertheless, my appetite wanes whenever I'm near this woman. Conversation is kept to a minimum because Veronika clears her throat every time someone starts to talk. A damn three quarters of an hour later, it's finally over. All courses have been served, everyone is full. Jessica and I express our thanks and make our exit. As we make our way upstairs to her room, I vow never to subject myself to another meal with the Flakes. In fact, I have no desire to be here at all. Whether Jess likes it or not, we'll spend the coming weeks exclusively at my place. I don't need to endure this crap. At least my girlfriend has calmed down, in the meantime. Good food works wonders on her.

"Hey, baby," she coos, leading me into her bedroom, "my butt is still all sticky from earlier. What do you say we hop into the shower together?"

"No thanks, I'll pass." The words come out harsher than I intended. I'm still irritated. "Sorry," I say conciliatorily because Jess isn't to blame. She didn't choose her mom. "What if you take a quick shower and then we head to the Brilliant for a bit?"

"No, I don't want to go to a club." The accurate phrasing would be: I don't want to go to that club. It's our team's favorite club - it's open every day except Mondays. Jess doesn't want to go to the Brilliant because she'll have to share me with the guys, that's clear. "How about a movie?" she suggests instead. Sliding my hands into my pockets, I shrug.

"Sure, why not." I'm fine with anything as long as I get out of here.

"Great. There's this incredibly heart-wrenching romance movie I've been wanting to see!" Fantastic. Jess claps her hands in excitement, gives me a quick peck on the corner of my mouth, and heads into the bathroom attached to her room.

Breaking the Ice

"I'll be quick!" I hear her call out, and the next moment, the water starts running.

"Take your time," I grumble, sitting on her bed and taking out my phone. To pass the time, I check my emails, Facebook, and Instagram. As usual, Jess takes forever. After half an hour, I start getting impatient and begin pacing around the room. I stop in front of her vanity mirror because I notice a photo of us. It shows us in front of my parents' house in Two Rivers, Wisconsin. Instantly, guilt washes over me. I reach for the picture frame to take a closer look at the photo. It was taken in spring, capturing a grinning Jessica leaning into me. My arm is casually draped over her shoulders, and the smile on my face is forced. Man, I was such an asshole. If Jessica knew that I originally added her on Facebook just because of her dad, she'd flip. But that's exactly what happened. I had learned that millionaire Carl Flake was on the hunt for hockey talents for his newly acquired team, the Portland Devils. I've been playing ice hockey since I was seven, and I love the sport. When I saw the article in the newspaper, I saw it as the chance of a lifetime. I was always a natural on the ice, but my problem was that I had never played in a higher league than our crappy school team. If I had just applied to Flake directly, he probably wouldn't have given me a second glance. So, I was convinced that I could win him over if I just had the opportunity to audition for him and demonstrate my skills. That's where Jessica came in. I messaged her, orchestrated a rapid infatuation, and visited her in Portland. A week later, the Devils provided me with an apartment and a car. Two weeks later, I helped the team achieve their first victory and was subsequently hailed as the new star forward. Half a year has passed since then, and much has happened. I've proven myself multiple times, taken the team far. Out of gratitude, I gave Jess a chance and didn't cast her aside once I achieved my goal. Somehow, I couldn't bring myself to do that. She was head over heels for me, so I gave it a shot. And wouldn't you know it, she grew on me. I'm aware that she's not the love of my life, nor will she be the mother of my children. But she's a good person, and she'll probably be by my side for a while longer.

Lost in thought, I run my thumb over the photo. My mom took it on the day I left. As much as I try to suppress my guilt towards Jess, it just won't go away. There's no excuse for knowingly using her - even if only initially. I lured her in with my looks, that's clear to me. Frowning, I examine the picture of myself more closely. I have sharp features, brown eyes, and a narrow nose. Personally, I prefer my teeth the most. They're naturally strikingly white. Jess, on the other hand, is more into my dark blond curls and my physique. Anyway, my appearance certainly opened the door to professional hockey. And I'm grateful for that.

"Ta-da!" I hear Jessica behind me. I turn to see her standing in the doorway to the bathroom, wearing a sky-blue dress. She's straightened her hip-length hair and put on makeup.

"Wow," I say approvingly, placing the picture frame back. "You look stunning." Okay, that's a bit exaggerated; even with all the makeup in the world, Jessica remains who she is - an average woman. But she does look pretty. "May I have this dance?" I ask, walking over to her and offering my arm for her to link with. "My lady has ordered a romantic movie night, and that's what she shall receive." And I mean that just the way I say it. Even if it means enduring a sappy romance flick. Jess deserves romance, and that's exactly what she'll get.

5

EMMA

"We should get proper beds as soon as possible. I feel completely drained," my dad laments, rolling his head back. He sits across from me at our tiny kitchen table, looking utterly exhausted. Dark circles lie beneath his eyes, and his hair resembles a bird's nest. He's slept on the sofa bed in the living room for my sake, giving me the single bed in the bedroom. Bill apologized numerous times yesterday for the sparsely furnished apartment, but given the short time frame, there wasn't much to be done. After all, it's only been two days since he got the job offer and we arrived. Mr. Flake insisted that we start as soon as possible.

"What do you think about hitting a few furniture stores later? Maybe we'll get lucky, and they'll deliver today," I suggest, taking a sip of my coffee from a glass tumbler. "And some dishes wouldn't hurt either. We don't have toilet paper or dish soap."

"True, I know. Apart from a carton of milk, the fridge is pretty empty. But that's not a problem; we have enough time to take care of everything. Today's training, if I remember correctly, is scheduled for late afternoon. Let me check." Dad

Breaking the Ice

reaches for a note lying behind him on the kitchen counter. He scans the training times written on it. "Today is Monday. Normally, the team would have training at eleven. But since they had a game yesterday..."

His index finger lands on the paper and slides down to a marginal note. "... It's postponed to five in the afternoon."

"Perfect. It's only eleven now. We have plenty of time to do the shopping without stress," I say with satisfaction, mentally compiling a list of all the things we need. My beeping phone grabs my attention. It's on the kitchen counter behind Dad.

"That's probably Riley," I explain as I get up. "I sent her a video of our new apartment earlier." Riley is my best friend. We've grown up together, known each other since kindergarten, and we're used to doing things together every day. It was tough for both of us when I got this job and had to pack up and move overnight.

While picking up the phone from the counter, I glance at the display. I was expecting a WhatsApp message, but instead, I find a text message. Odd. I open the message from an unfamiliar number and read the following sentence:

11:30 A.M. in the massage room. Need a treatment.

Frowning, I return to my seat and sit down. What a rude text. There isn't even a name mentioned. Well, who knows. Brief messages are probably common among professionals, I consider. Time is money, after all.

"What's up?" Dad looks at me over the edge of his newspaper, which he's just opened. "Is something wrong with Riley?"

"No, but I received a text from one of the players."

"Oh yeah? From whom?"

"It doesn't say."

"And what does the mysterious man write?"

"Basically, just that he needs a treatment at 11:30."

"That's in less than half an hour, and you haven't even had

Breaking the Ice

a proper breakfast. I'll take care of it for you," he suggests, setting the newspaper aside.

"No, Dad, it's fine, I don't mind."

"Are you sure?"

"Absolutely," I assure him, getting up and heading to the bedroom to change. I exchange the oversized T-shirt I'm wearing for a mint-green polo shirt with the words "Tade – Healing Hands" embroidered over the chest. I slip into white pants and sneakers. Then I head to the bathroom, tying my shoulder-length black hair into a ponytail. This will be my first official treatment. I'm immensely excited, a feeling mirrored on my face. My slightly uneven dark brown eyes seem to gleam. I owe my eye shape to Mom, just as I do my flawless skin. She's Thai by birth and... oh man, I haven't even had time to call her yet. I resolve to give her a detailed report later in the evening. It must be tough for her to be home alone in Aberdeen without Dad and me.

With no time to spare, my makeup is minimal – just some eyeliner to accentuate my cat-like eyes and a bit of mascara. I spend a little more time brushing my teeth, as neglecting oral hygiene is something I find repulsive. After spitting out the toothpaste and wiping away the foam, I return to the kitchen where Dad is still engrossed in his newspaper.

"Sure you don't want me to take over?" he asks.

"Dad, stop worrying. I've got this!" I retrieve my jacket from the back of the chair, grab the key to the company car we've been provided, and plant a kiss on his forehead. "I need to go, see you later. Love you!" Without waiting for his response, I hurry away. I'm running late.

Four minutes before half past eleven, I arrive breathless in my massage room. Traffic on Portland's streets is horrendous around noon, I've come to realize. Fortunately, the player who requested my services seems to be running late too, as I'm the only one here. That's fine by me; it gives me a moment to acclimate. I switch on the light, take off my jacket, and hang it on the hook on the wall behind the oil shelf. Then I step into the adjacent bathroom to wash my hands. Since I didn't get a chance to look around in here yesterday, I let my gaze wander through the small space. Toward the front is a sink and a shelf with towels. Further back, next to a shower, there's a toilet. The room, much like the team's locker room, is tiled in white, and, as I notice, equipped with underfloor heating. On the left wall, the grinning devil's face of the Devils is plastered above a few hooks. *They must be quite patriotic here, the logo is everywhere,* I think to myself, just as I sense something behind me. I turn around and spot a guy watching me near the massage table.

"Oh, hi," I greet him, wondering if he's the player who summoned me. I can't recall seeing him with the others when Bill introduced me yesterday. I would have remembered that face!

"Hi," he replies curtly, his baritone voice filling the room.

"Have you been standing there for long?" I ask. For some reason, he makes me nervous. The way he's studying me with those dark eyes feels eerie.

"No," he answers matter-of-factly, and I don't know why, but I'm certain he's lying.

"Okay, so I assume you sent me the text message," I say, feeling apprehensive, and move toward him. "I'm Emma," I introduce myself as I stand before the man, who's about six-foot-three, and extend my hand. I don't want him to sense my insecurity, so I smile at him nonchalantly.

"Caleb," he says, shaking my hand. The sensation of his warm skin against mine is almost uncomfortably intense, causing me to retract my hand quickly. This has never happened to me in my twenty-one years.

"Okay, so you need a massage?"

Breaking the Ice

"Yeah, I'm about to head to the weight room." While Caleb speaks, I position myself casually at the head of the massage table – putting some safe distance between us. I don't know what it is, but this man has something about him that makes me nervous. Maybe it's his voice, which slips beneath my skin stealthily, like a mosquito bite. Or maybe it's the way he's looking at me. With that gaze that conceals his thoughts. He definitely irritates me, and I don't like it. No one can easily throw me off balance; then why am I reacting this way to him?

"Which muscle group are you planning to work on?"

"I'm working on my legs."

"Particularly the calf muscles, I presume?"

"Among other things, yes."

"Alright, please take off your jeans and socks and lie down," I say, gesturing toward the bathroom, and turn to the oil shelf. As I search for a circulation-enhancing oil, I hear him unfastening his belt behind me. The sound sends a shiver down my spine. *What's he doing? Why is he changing in here with me?* I turn to face him, about to suggest the bathroom, when he sits on the massage table and lies down on his back. Out of courtesy and because it's a golden rule in my profession, I avoid looking at his intimate region. "I actually meant for you to lie on your stomach," I say, prompting him with my suggestion, as he gives me an expectant brow furrow.

"Patrick always started face up." And from Caleb's tone, it seems he insists on keeping it that way, I note. What's his problem? Why is he acting this way? Is he trying to provoke me? Even if he is, I won't let it affect me. Mr. Flake demands that his guys get what they want. So fine, I'll adapt. I force a smile and approach him at the table. Keeping my back to him, I stand at hip height next to him and put some oil on my hand. It carries a faint scent of arnica. Then I place both hands on his right thigh. The touch triggers a fluttering sensation in my chest, which I ignore. With smooth strokes, I work my way down his muscular leg. Caleb says nothing, and I stay silent too. Instead, there's an electric tension in the air between us. Who knows, maybe I'm just sleep-deprived and emotionally unstable as a result.

Minutes pass as I force myself to concentrate on my work. As I stand at the foot of the table to attend to his feet, allowing him to see my face, he unexpectedly initiates a conversation.

"So, you and your dad are new to the city?"

I lift my head, meeting his inquiring gaze.

"We arrived yesterday, yes."

"And where are you from?"

"Aberdeen."

"How old are you?"

"Twenty-one."

"Did the Devils provide you with an apartment?"

"Yes." What's with this interrogation? First, he barely says a word, and now he's bombarding me with questions out of nowhere.

"And a car?"

Okay, what's this supposed to be? Your own one-man quiz show? Sorry, buddy, that's not going to work with me; It's time to turn the tables.

"Yep, that was part of it. We need to be available at all times. What about you? You're not from Portland, I can tell by your accent. Where are you from?"

"Two Rivers. And do you have family and friends back in Aberdeen?"

"Loads of them. But I'm sure you can relate, right? It probably wasn't any different for you," I remark, my hands pausing in their motion – I've stopped massaging. Instead, I'm giving him a challenging look.

"And did you leave a boyfriend behind?"

Breaking the Ice

Caleb's directness borders on impudence. I'm about to answer when he continues, "I'm sure someone like you is already taken, right?" The guy seriously has a nerve. And I'm just as guilty because somewhere deep in my subconscious, a voice wonders what it would be like to be his girlfriend. That's insane, though! Why am I thinking something so absurd? I don't have, nor do I want, a boyfriend. Life is too short to be bothered with men. No, I'd rather just flirt with them and spare myself the relationship drama.

"Are you always this straightforward?" I steer around his question. After all, it's none of his business whether I'm taken or not.

"Most of the time."

"So, I guess your approach is 'shoot first, ask questions later'?"

"Usually." Caleb seems unfazed by my response, which makes me want to twist his toes.

"Alright now, do you have a boyfriend?"

"What about you, do you have a girlfriend?"

"Yes, I do." His response comes quickly. By now, I'm sure that I must be sleep-deprived, as I feel a faint disappointment welling up inside me. That's definitely not normal and must be due to my lack of sleep. I really should lie down!

"No, I don't have a boyfriend."

"Then the men in Aberdeen are either blind or gay." Under different circumstances, I'd say the guy is flirting with me in the most impertinent way possible. But Caleb's words don't sound like a pickup line; rather, they sound like an observation.

"I'll take that as a compliment. So, thank you," I say, furrowing my brow, adding a bit more oil and continuing the massage on his other foot.

"Not a problem. I'm pretty sure most of the team agrees

with me."

"I see," I say with a smile.

"By the way, you've left quite an impression on some of them. They'll be pleased to hear you're not taken." Parker comes to mind, how he visited me here yesterday and flirted. *I get it now, that's the deal.*

"Are you here to pry into me for one of the others?"

"No, they manage that just fine on their own." He props himself up on his elbows, and I see his abdominal muscles working beneath the tight shirt. For a tiny moment, I weaken, and my gaze slips a bit lower to the dark shorts with a noticeable bulge. *What is it with these hockey players? Are they all so loaded or what? Durand yesterday, Caleb today, this isn't normal!* "I'm here because I want to know if you can handle the guys."

"What do you mean?"

"Some of the players are unpredictable hotshots, and I can't afford disruption in the team." Ah, I finally get it. Caleb Whyler is the captain of the Devils. I read that in Dad's team files yesterday. I knew I recognized the name from somewhere. So, as captain, he's worried I might pit his players against each other.

"Don't worry, I don't plan on getting involved with any of them," I say. *At least not in terms of sex or a relationship. As far as I'm concerned that topic is closed,* so I refocus my attention on his feet.

"I'm just afraid that won't stop them. You'll see, they'll try to get your attention in every possible way."

"Please, let them." I don't have a problem with that. *On the contrary, a few flirts will make my time here more enjoyable. But he doesn't need to know that.* "Caleb," I say, because his expression darkens, and I don't want to sour things with him. "You really don't need to worry. I'm here to work, not to cause discord in your team." For a moment, he looks at me assessingly. In that moment, my heart thumps unusually hard against my ribcage, confusing me. *Am I afraid he won't believe me, or is it the deep brown of his eyes, the way he looks at me, that's accelerating my pulse?*

"Alright," is all he says before lying down again, and I start working on his thighs. A few minutes later, I ask him to turn onto his stomach so I can continue on his back. I notice that he has an incredibly hot butt. In fact, this man has an amazing physique. And hey, it means something when I say that, because he's not the first athlete I've seen in minimal clothing.

He remains silent for the rest of the massage, which suits me fine. There's a kind of tension between us. But I notice that with each touch—running my hands over his skin—that tension diminishes a bit. When I finally finish, Caleb even looks relaxed.

"Alright, that's it," I explain and run my hands over his calves one last time. "Your muscles are warmed up and well blooded. It's best if you head to practice."

"Got it, thanks." His voice sounds rough, as if he just woke up. While Caleb sits up, I go to the bathroom to wash the oil off my hands.

"By the way," I say, looking at the hockey player who's just getting up from the table and pushing his chin-length curls back, "for next time: you don't need to change out there. There are hooks in here."

"I know," he says and reaches for his clothes that he laid on the dresser. *He knows? And yet he still changes in the massage room? Odd bird.*

"Then I don't need to worry that the guys will bash each other's skulls in because of you?" he asks again as I return to him. He's standing fully dressed next to the table, rolling up the sleeves of his long-sleeved shirt. The dark blond hair, the sharp facial features, and then those intelligent eyes. Oh man,

Breaking the Ice

I have to admit, Caleb looks delicious. If anyone on the team could truly tempt me, it's him. But I stay away from men who are taken. Fishing in unfamiliar waters isn't my thing.

"As I said, I don't intend to get involved with any of them."

"Good." That serious expression returns to his face as he nods and heads to the door. I turn my attention to the table, about to remove the linen cover to prepare it for the next client when Caleb—his hand on the doorknob—pauses. He turns around to face me once more, seeking my gaze.

"Thank you," he says, and for the first time, I think I see a hint of a smile at the corners of his mouth.

"No problem."

"And welcome to the Devils." With that, he presses the doorknob and disappears into the hallway.

6

CALEB

As I close the door to the massage room behind me and walk down the corridor, I can't help but think, *What a woman.* Parker was right; Emma is stunning. Her face is flawlessly beautiful. The petite nose, high cheekbones, and those cat-like eyes. I bet she's hiding an amazing figure under that simple cotton pants and shirt. Damn, if I could design a woman, she'd look just like her. She's way too good for Durand, that poser. And even though Parker is my best friend and I want him to have a pretty woman, this one is out of his league. Celebrity status or not. It's pretty intense, but even though I had sex this morning and I'm satisfied, it was a challenge not to get aroused under Emma's delicate hands. If Jess knew what a smoking hot masseuse Bill hired, she'd flip. Better to keep them from meeting. Otherwise, my girlfriend would lose her mind, that's for sure. Speaking of Jessica, I have a lunch date with her at one. That's in less than an hour. I should hurry up with my workout.

As I push myself in the weight room, Emma's image keeps popping into my head. The dimples at the corners of her mouth when she smiles, or the sparkle in her eyes when suspicion sets in. Thinking about how her gentle hands felt on my skin, I accidentally drop a dumbbell inches away from my foot. Shit! Before I injure myself in my absentmindedness, I call it quits on the training. Hydrating with the water bottle, I have with me; I head back to the locker room.

"Hey, Whyler, how's it going?" I'm greeted by Parker, sitting in front of his locker with his gym bag between his legs. A grin stretches across his face from ear to ear.

"What are you doing here at this time?" I ask him, surprised. "The training doesn't start until five."

"Oh, I just wanted to hit the weight room a bit early," he says, making me raise an eyebrow. Parker voluntarily in the weight room? No way! He hates lifting weights or pedaling more than any of us. Then I remember what Carl said last night. He insists that his three strongest players, Durand, Parker, and me, get massages daily.

"Let me guess. You're here less for the training and more for the bet, right?"

"What can I say? Flake got me a free flirt with our little masseuse. He wants me to see her every day to avoid strains and stuff. So, I booked an appointment for one o'clock."

"I see." Well, tough luck for him, he won't score with Emma. "What time is it, by the way?"

"Quarter to one, why?"

"Damn! I'm meeting Jess. Sorry, buddy, gotta run, catch you later," I say as I grab my shower gel from the locker and hurry out to the corridor leading to the showers.

★★★

"Apologies, babe. Traffic getting here was insane," I lie as I arrive at Passo, our favorite Mexican restaurant, with a twenty-minute delay. Carrying my motorcycle helmet in hand, I

Breaking the Ice

approach my girlfriend, who's waiting for me at our usual spot, a cozy corner booth. My words make her look up from her phone, and her features light up when she sees me.

"Hey, sweetheart, there you are," she greets me with a smile.

"Did you already order?" I ask as I take a seat next to her and place the helmet under the table.

"No, I wanted to wait for you." Her grumbling stomach fuels my guilt.

"Sorry."

"It's alright, you're here now." She leans over to give me a kiss on the lips and signals the waiter to come over. We order our usual. Two Pepsis, a Quesadilla for Jess, and a Yucateca steak with grilled vegetables for me.

"So, spill the beans, what's there to discuss?" I ask once the waiter is out of earshot. I know Jess. If she wants to meet me for lunch during the week, something's on her mind.

"Ooooh," she squeals, clenching her fists in excitement. "It's about Professor Weinstein."

"Is that the one who loved your paintings?" Jess is an art student at Reed College. She's a talented illustrator with an incredible eye for detail.

"Uh-huh. He called them outstanding." Stress marks of excitement appear on Jessica's cheeks. "Listen up! He's planning to organize an exhibition for his top three students. And, Caleb, he asked if I want to be part of it. Me!" She squeaks again, practically lunging at me in excitement, almost knocking over the candle in the center of the table.

"That's fantastic. I'm so happy for you. You deserve it."

"Yeah, right? I really do," she says, nodding and releasing me from her embrace. "I mean, I'm top of the class. Just the nude I painted recently..."

While Jess raves about her works, my thoughts drift to Emma. Parker probably hit on her throughout the entire mas-

Breaking the Ice

sage. A mental image forms in my mind. I see Emma's delicate fingers spreading warm oil on my buddy's legs and tenderly stroking his skin.

"Caleb? Caleb?!" I blink as my girlfriend looks at me with a furrowed brow, clearly annoyed. "Are you even listening to me?"

"Of course, I'm listening to you." The waiter who's just brought our drinks saves me. As he places the ice-cold Pepsis in front of us, I reach for my girlfriend's hand and give it a reassuring squeeze, dissipating her anger. "Alright," she continues as soon as we're alone again. "Susanna and Martin are my two competitors, you could say. They're the other two who get to participate in the exhibition. Mr. Weinstein said…"

I wonder if Durand has already made a move on Emma. No, I don't think he'd take that approach to get to her. He's more of a dating type. I pick up my Pepsi and wash away the sour taste the thought of Durand and Emma conjures.

My attention is diverted again as the waiter brings our food. While I savor my steak, my girlfriend is too excited to eat anything. Instead, she fills me in on her latest plan. She wants her father to buy some of her paintings for the exhibition. She thinks it would impress Mr. Weinstein. Meanwhile, I contemplate whether I should let Emma in on the bet. *The guys would probably give me a hard time if they found out, but it might be worth it. Or not? Ah, well, Emma is smart; she'll probably figure it out on her own soon.*

"Caleb, damn it!" Jessica's hand hitting the table startles me. Damn, I've zoned out again.

"Sorry, what did you say?" I cross my arms as she shoots me an annoyed look, her blue eyes narrowing.

"I was asking if you could help me transport the paintings. What's going on with you today?"

I should really engage more in her excitement about the

upcoming exhibition. "I'm sorry, I didn't mean to be rude. I just didn't sleep well last night and I'm a bit out of it, that's all. Of course, I'll help you with the paintings. It goes without saying," I say, flashing my apologetic smile. Then I take her hand and plant a kiss on her knuckles, which quickly softens her mood.

The rest of the meal, I make a conscious effort to pay attention to Jess and her chatter. Afterward, I head home to my loft for some downtime before heading to practice at the ice rink around four.

The locker room is as chaotic as ever. Twenty guys cramming themselves into gear, talking over one another, and laughing. Everyone's dressed except for Toby. He stands shirtless in front of Byers, one of our defensemen, a dark-skinned guy. Toby points to his own chest. "This, my friend, is my little love jungle. Women dig it, I'm telling you."

"Love jungle! You're out of your mind! You look like a yeti."

"What do you mean yeti? If anything, I'm a bear. Balu the Bear – king of the jungle," Toby says, rubbing his hairy chest provocatively.

"I'm gonna puke," Byers mutters as he squeezes past the massive Swiss guy to take his seat and put on his skates. "Balu the Bear? I'm gonna throw up!"

"Kid, you have no clue about women. They love hairy men, believe me. All they need to do is run their fingers through my jungle, and they're aroused. And then it's like, lift the skirt, insert the stick."

Europeans and their humor, I think, shaking my head, and I go over to my locker. As I change, I glance over at Parker, who's slipping on his gloves. He doesn't look particularly cheerful, so I suspect Emma turned him down. Sorry for him... Okay, no, I'm not sorry. But he really did gamble too high on that one. Durand is nowhere to be seen. I wonder where the Canadian is. Ten minutes later, as I step onto the ice fully dressed, I get my answer. He's already training. As I do a few laps to warm up, I keep an eye on him. He looks as usual. I contemplate mentioning the bet to him, asking how things are going. I'm really curious whether he's seen Emma today. That pretty arrogant boy is hard to read. Just as I'm about to skate over to him and strike up a conversation, the shrill sound of Coach Thornton's whistle slices through the air.

"Alright, guys, gather up!" shouts the small man from the center of the ice. He stands with some papers in his hand. "We've got a game against the Iron Hawks on Saturday. Those guys have top-notch defense and a forward who's supposed to give Whyler a run for his money."

"Bullshit! No one's as good as Whyler," Parker chimes in, and the rest of the team confirms his words by thumping their sticks on the ice three times in a row. It's a tribute to my first game where I scored three goals and sent our then toughest opponents home with a three-to-one loss.

"Anyways, I want you guys well prepared. Warm up and then I want Byers, Hard, and the rest of the defense on the north side," Thornton's finger points to the upper area of the rink where some pucks lie. I understand what that means – he'll be training their agility, making them do slaloms. "The rest of you focus on Toby. I want him sweating." He gestures toward the net on the south side. "Now, let's get moving!"

Thornton's shrill whistle goes off again, and we start skating, warming up.

Shortly after, our Swiss goalie takes his place in front of the net, and we line up in front of him. As usual, he signals a kiss, pressing it first onto his massive glove and then onto the red goal frame. The guy is off the wall. He's named his net – Samantha. And Samantha is his everything. Heaven help anyone who gets too close to his 'sweetie'. He actually lost it

Breaking the Ice

in a game once when an opponent tore Samantha from her moorings. He's a freak, no doubt about it. But he's a freak who damn well keeps his 'box', as we call it, clean.

"Ready to go, losers?" Toby calls to us as he gets ready, crouching slightly. Parker goes first, shooting, but our goalie easily blocks it. The next three pucks don't make it past him either. "What, is that all you've got?!" he taunts, prompting Durand to put in extra effort. But neither he nor I manage to score. "You guys are such pussies! My grandma plays better. Maybe I should bring her in to show you how to score!"

Fired up by his comment, we intensify the pressure on the Swiss goalie, firing shots at him in increasingly rapid succession. He's struggling, panting heavily like a walrus. "All good, Samy-Baby, all good," I hear him groan after Parker's final shot, which he almost missed. That's it, I think, we've got him now, he's getting tired. And sure enough, my next shot sails past him and smacks into the net. The black rubber puck clatters onto the ice.

"What's the matter, Toby? Should we call your grandma to show you how it's done?" I taunt him, then turn to Parker, signaling for him to follow up. But as I glance toward Durand, who's standing by the boards, he turns away from the ice. He's leaning casually against the open bench door, leading to the locker room. *What's he doing there?* As I'm about to skate over and check on him, my attention lands on the bench. Damn it! Wrapped in a thick coat and wearing a white beanie, Emma is sitting there, watching our practice. And of course, that slimy bastard is taking advantage of the situation, hitting on her. Just wait! I grab a puck, skate to the blue line, and fire it straight at Durand's ass with all my might. Even though he's wearing protective gear, he yelps as the puck hits him. He turns toward me immediately. But before he can say anything, Thornton spots him leaning against the boards. If there's one thing our coach can't stand, it's lazy players.

"Durand!" he bellows across the ice. Through the grid visor of his helmet, I can see the Canadian's face contort in reaction. "Come over here, now!"

"Yeah, Coach?" Durand's face twists and he shoots me a just-you-wait-I'll-get-you-for-this look.

"Get over here, now!" Thornton commands. While the coach reads him the riot act, I seize the opportunity to skate over to Emma.

"Hey, how's it going? Everything alright?" I ask. Oh man, she looks incredibly cute in that cream-colored coat and the pom-pom beanie. She directs her amused gaze toward me, warming me from the inside.

"Everything's fine. I just wanted to see what a training session looks like for you guys."

"I see," I say with a lopsided grin, realizing that she probably saw my recent goal. "Maybe you'd like to..."

"Whyler!" Dammit. I narrow my eyes. Thornton's spotted me. "What the hell are you doing? Get over here immediately!"

"Sorry," I say to Emma, who bites her lip and looks back and forth between me and Thornton. "I have to go. See you later." She nods, gracing me with a smile that almost throws me off balance.

"See you, Caleb," she says, raising a gloved hand.

"Damn it," I mutter as I skate back to Thornton and a smug-looking Durand.

7

EMMA

With a sigh, I collapse onto the couch in the living room. It's Saturday afternoon, I've completed my first week of work, and I feel utterly drained. I never thought my new job could be so exhausting. Unlike me, Dad, sitting next to me in his new armchair, seems to be bursting with energy. *Well, he's used to massaging for several hours a day,* I think. Besides, he didn't have nearly as much to do this week as I did. All 22 players wanted massages from me. At first, I felt honored, I enjoyed getting to know the guys, and flirting with a few of them. But by the third day, I was just completely exhausted. My legs ached from standing all the time, and my fingers were swollen like sausages. *No wonder after all those massages.* For the past two days, I've been walking around on autopilot due to exhaustion. Yesterday, I fell asleep during the drive home. Dad carried me into the apartment and into my new bed. We had to make do with the folding couch and the squeaky bed until Thursday because the furniture store couldn't deliver sooner. It doesn't matter, as long as the stuff is finally here.

Yawning, I glance at my wristwatch. It's almost three in the afternoon. The frozen pizzas I put in the oven for us still need

Breaking the Ice

ten more minutes. An eternity, I think, rubbing my burning eyes.

"Should I make you some coffee?" Dad asks, holding the remote control in his hand, looking over at me. A crease of concern forms between his brows, digging vertically into his forehead.

"No, thanks. I think I'll just go to bed and lie down for an hour," I reply, swaying as I get up.

"Now? Already?" he asks in surprise as I struggle to stand.

"Yeah, otherwise I'll fall asleep sitting here."

"And what about the pizza? You didn't have dinner last night, and I think you only had that bagel for breakfast today."

"And a chocolate bar while I was waiting for Toby after the game," I concede, giving in to Dad's stern expression. "I'll eat the pizza later when I wake up, okay?"

"But it'll be cold."

"I don't mind." When it comes to cold food, he's just like Mom. 'A warm meal a day is a must for humans,' is her motto, and Dad is in full agreement. But if I wait for the pizza to finish cooking, I'll get over the tiredness, or worse, feel sick from it. "See you later," I say, giving my father a kiss on the cheek. Before he starts on the tiresome topic of 'you're not eating enough', I make my way to my room. It's still sparsely furnished, housing only a queen-sized bed and a wardrobe. But that doesn't bother me in the slightest. Even if I had just a mattress on the floor, I'd be content. The main thing is having a place to sleep. Rubbing my sore neck, I kick off my sneakers and slip out of my clothes, sliding under the covers. My ears are ringing, as if I've just come home from a nightclub. How can one be so exhausted? I grab my phone to set the alarm when I notice four new WhatsApp messages. All of them are from the 'Portland Devils' group. Parker added me earlier this week. He said all the Devils' team members are in it, which

Breaking the Ice

isn't true. Besides the players and me, I found only their former masseur, Patrick, and a couple of numbers I don't recognize in the group info. Curious as I am, I open the messages.

Byers writes:

Hey guys, we really dominated the Iron Hawks today. 5:1! Incredible game!

Toby responds:

We tore those pussies apart, that's what happened!

Parker:

This calls for a celebration. Tonight, at the Brillant! Emma, you in?

Even though my eyes are about to close, I can't help but laugh. I can picture Parker right in front of me, his ice-blue eyes focused on his phone screen, waiting for my reply.

Durand:

Yes, Emma, we insist that you come. After all, you're our new good luck charm.

The good luck charm thing is complete nonsense. But hockey players are superstitious, that's just how they are. In today's game, the Devils were trailing 0-1 until the second period when I showed up to watch. From that point on, as they claimed, the game turned around. Durand, Parker, and Caleb were scoring goal after goal. Anyway, they're a step closer to the playoffs thanks to this victory, and from now on, I'm officially their good luck charm. Another WhatsApp notification vibrates my phone. This time it's a private message from Durand.

Thanks to you, I scored my tenth goal of the season today. Allow me to invite you for a drink in gratitude. How about tonight around nine at the Brillant?

Well, well, well, I think, feeling a grin tug at my lips. All week, Durand has been flirting with me. Not in the blatant way Parker does, seizing every opportunity to chat me up.

Breaking the Ice

No, Durand is more of a guy who flirts with his eyes—from a distance. He intentionally keeps his distance, doesn't reveal much. That's what makes him even more intriguing. And he's well aware of that. It's his style. A style that, I have to admit, I'm liking. I think he's not the unsympathetic show-off I initially thought he was.

Nibbling on my lower lip, I consider how to reply.

*Congratulations on your tenth goal. I'll come by to celebrate the next ten with you.

Even though it's not the most original answer, I send it. My mind is too empty for anything better. After that, I set the alarm on my phone for six o'clock, settle into the pillows, and succumb to sleep.

My father's agitated voice rouses me from a deep slumber. Blinking groggily, it takes me a moment to realize I'm in my bed. Judging by Dad's muffled voice, he must be outside in the hallway. I sit up and see nothing but darkness seeping through the slats of the window blind. *Crap, what time is it?* I glance at my phone. It's almost half past seven. *Damn, I slept through the whole afternoon.* And now I see why. What an idiot I am—I set the alarm for Sunday instead of Saturday.

"You should have thought about that sooner," I hear my father hiss outside in the hallway. I wonder who he's talking to? I narrow my eyes and listen, but I don't hear a second voice. That's odd. Judging by the creaking of the floorboards, he's heading toward the kitchen. If he's wandering around the apartment, he must be on the phone, as he can never sit still during phone calls. But that doesn't explain his tense tone. I need to know what's going on! I quickly put on the clothes I tossed carelessly on the floor and sneak out of my room towards the kitchen.

"I don't know how many times I have to tell you this. I don't care, do you hear me? I don't care at all." I stop in the doorway, peering into the room. Dad is leaning against the sink, his back turned, squeezing the bridge of his nose, listening to the voice on the other end.

"No," he replies, still not opening his eyes. "Because it's pointless. That's why." He listens to the voice on the other end for a moment, then shakes his head and lifts his eyelids. "You know what, let's talk another time. I've got something to do." With those words, he runs a hand through his black hair, now graying at the temples, with a sigh. The pained expression on his face tightens my chest. Worried, I step into the room. When Dad spots me, he suddenly turns pale. "I have to go, we'll talk later," he says, ending the call. "Emma, sweetheart, you're finally awake," his voice sounds unusually thin, as if he has a lump in his throat. "I was beginning to think you'd sleep through the whole day."

"Who was that on the phone?" I ask.

"Nobody important."

"That sounded different. What's the matter, Dad?"

"Oh, it's really unimportant. It was just... Mike, you know, the janitor from my massage practice in Aberdeen."

"And what did he want?" With my arms crossed, I give him a suspicious look. I didn't get the feeling that he was talking to Mike. As far as I know, they hardly know each other.

"It was about a burst pipe in the practice. The toilet had a leak, and Mike took care of it. But instead of fixing it, he damaged the drainage pipe. He said he'd sort it out. But I mean, a real plumber should look at it, not a janitor." He shrugs. "I just don't want to come back to a place that stinks of sewage after the season. You understand, right?"

"I can understand, yes." My answer brings a smile to his lips.

"Good. And now, about you. I put your pizza..." The ringing of his phone interrupts him. For a split second, I see an an-

Breaking the Ice

gry expression flash across his face. Then he recognizes who's calling and smiles. "Just a moment, okay?" he says, turning to me, and answers the call. "Hey, Bill, what's up?" While I walk to the fridge to get some water, Dad goes from the kitchen to the living room to take the call. He seems more at ease now, not as downcast.

"Is everything okay?" I inquire as I gulp down water, before taking a large bite of my Diavolo pizza, covered with a generous amount of barbecue sauce.

"How can you eat that artificial stuff?" he dodges, gesturing toward the bottle.

"It tastes good," I mumble, in between mouthfuls. Plus, it's spicy, and I'm into that. Growing up with a Thai mother, I'm used to spicy food. "What did Bill want?" I ask as soon as I've swallowed.

"He convinced me to go have a drink with him. You know, to celebrate the Devils' win today. And since they don't have practice tomorrow and we're off, I figured I'd say yes." Why is he talking so fast? In fact, he's been acting strange since I woke up. "It's not a problem if I go out, is it?" Okay, now it's official, he's acting weird.

"Of course not. Why would it bother me?"

"I don't know... because, well, because you'd be here alone." He looks at me apologetically.

"Dad, I'm an adult and perfectly capable of handling myself. You don't need to worry about me." *Plus*, I think to myself, *Durand is waiting for me at the Brillant*. I wasn't sure whether to go there or not. But now that even my dad is going out, even though he usually stays at home all year, it's like a sign. "Besides," I continue, "I was planning to meet up with the others later."

"The others? You mean the players?"

Wow, why is he suddenly so serious? Dad's mood has shift-

Breaking the Ice

ed from neutral to alarmed in the blink of an eye. His voice has dropped by an octave, and a worried expression has taken over his eyes.

"Of course, the players. Who else would I meet up with? I don't really know anyone else here."

"Did you hear what they did to our predecessor, Patrick?"

"What they did to him? That sounds like they forced him or something." I can hardly believe they forced Patrick into drinking. As far as I know, he's thirty. At that age, you should know your limits.

"Maybe, but you're only twenty-one." *Wait, what? Is he implying that just because I'm young, I don't know when to stop?* I raise my brows in disbelief, prompting him to backtrack. He raises his hands. "I'm not saying you're not responsible. I'm just thinking, for a pretty girl like you, it's dangerous to hang out with the players."

"I was planning on going out anyway. And rather than wandering around Portland's nightlife all alone, it's smarter for me to be with the guys." My father doesn't respond to that, just grumbles something incomprehensible to himself. "What was that?"

"Oh, nothing. Eat your pizza before it gets cold." With two steps, he's at my table, planting a kiss on my forehead. "I won't be gone long. Definitely take your phone with you, and call if you need anything."

"I will," I promise, "and now go and have a nice evening with Bill."

"Got it." Dad grabs his faux-leather jacket hanging over the back of his chair and slips it on. It looks great on him, making him appear years younger. Overall, with his brown eyes framed by thick brows, the five o'clock shadow, and his full head of hair, he's a good-looking man. "Oh, before I forget," he says, pulling the car keys from his pants pocket, "you can use the car; I'll take a taxi." Now I can't help but chuckle. Dad only lets me have the car for one reason: he wants me to avoid drinking. Although I have no intention of driving, I'll take a taxi like him. If I'm going out, I want to enjoy something alcoholic. I spare him this info and instead wish him a good evening.

As the apartment door closes behind my father, I stand up and head to my room. While I rummage through the closet for a suitable outfit for the Brillant, I call my friend Riley. Let's see what's new with her and her quarterback, Cole.

8

CALEB

"Hey, check out this pussy squeezer," Toby shouts over the noise of the disco. His finger blatantly points at a blonde passing beneath our VIP area. She's wearing a glittery top and tight jeans, revealing the outline of her labia.

"A prime camel toe," Parker replies with a laugh.

"I find it hot. At least you know what you're getting," the Swiss guy comments, giving the girl a suggestive eyebrow wiggle and an air kiss. The blonde smiles but hesitates to pass the two security guards blocking the VIP area. "Always the same with these gorillas," Toby complains. "They scare away all the young birds."

"If you like her, then go and talk to her," I suggest.

He waves it off. "Nah, forget it. I'm too lazy to get up."

What nonsense, I think. *Toby isn't lazy at all; he's just scared.* Despite having the biggest mouth among us, he struggles to approach women he's interested in. He's decent at casual flirting, but when it comes to a real conversation, he suddenly loses his words.

"Whatever you say," I reply, patting his leg and rising from the white leather couch. The thing is massive, taking up the en-

Breaking the Ice

tire length of the VIP area wall. This section of the Brillant club is slightly elevated, providing a perfect view from the couch.

"Hey, what's this? Are you planning to make a move on the blonde? Just so you know, I spotted her first!" Toby's huge hand grabs my leg, holding me back.

"Man, you freak, chill out! I'm not interested in the girl. Don't forget, I have a girlfriend," I explain, shaking him off and heading towards the security guys. When they notice me, one of them releases the red velvet rope and lets me through. Running my fingers through my hair, I descend the three steps leading to the public area. Even though it's only shortly after nine, the Brillant is bustling. On my way to the restroom, I scan my surroundings. Except for the couch, the VIP area's chairs, and the four white bars located in each corner of the club, everything inside is black. This amplifies the effect of the club's centerpiece, the dance floor. It's round and made of a special glass that resembles the surface of a diamond. Depending on how the light hits the glass, it shatters and scatters into hundreds of sparkling color specks, just like a real gemstone. A real eye-catcher. Just like the podium with the two pole-dance poles right behind the dance floor, below the DJ booth. According to Parker, this place used to be a high-end strip joint. The owner miscalculated the profits and had to sell. The stripper poles are the only reminder of that time. They're new, made of the same special glass as the dance floor. The Brillant might not be the biggest club in Portland, but its setup is definitely unique.

Outside the restroom, I'm intercepted by two pushy women who claim to be my biggest fans. They get up close, urging me to give them an autograph. Knowing I won't be able to shake them off until I fulfill their request, I give them my signature on their collarbones. Then I make my escape from their intrusive hands and alcohol breath. Finally in the restroom,

Breaking the Ice

I stand irritably in front of a urinal. *What the hell am I doing here? Why did I let Parker convince me to come with him? I could be relaxing at home in my loft right now. Or screwing Jess's brains out and spilling all over her tits.* The thought of spreading my cum across her boobs makes my cock twitch in my hand. I definitely need a decent fuck tonight. That's for sure. On days when we're behind in a game and then catch up and win, I'm always particularly horny. It's as if the tension releases a special testosterone charge in my balls. Anyway, the evening already feels too long for me. And it's only just begun. Maybe I should lie, tell the guys that Jess is having one of her jealous fits again and make my escape. At least that wouldn't surprise anyone. They know Jessica, know that she can be demanding in that way. I tuck my meat back into my jeans and step to one of the sinks. As I wash my hands, I look at my reflection in the mirror, the face that clearly shows my bad mood. My lips form a tight line, and there's a dark look around my eyes. *Come on, Caleb, pull yourself together,* a voice in my head whispers, *it's been ages since you've gone out with Parker. Jessica isn't going anywhere; you can fuck her all night.* I nod silently to my thoughts, straighten my shirt collar and jacket, and head back outside. The annoying girls from earlier are gone. At least that's something. I push through the crowd toward the VIP area. As usual around this time, it's getting more crowded by the minute. As I pass the dance floor, a strange feeling washes over me. It's like a cool breeze brushing against me. The hairs on my arms stand on end. Before I realize what's happening, I see her. Emma. She stands about five meters away from me in an off-the-shoulder white dress that clings to her body like a second skin, looking around searchingly. My breath gets caught in my throat as I lay eyes on her. This woman is drop-dead gorgeous. I watch as she tucks her black hair, gleaming like silk in the dim light, behind her ear. Clearly, she's not only catching my eye because the guy next to her turns to address her. Anger rises within me as I see him offer her a cocktail glass and casually touch her upper arm. Just as I'm about to walk over and chase the jerk away, Durand appears beside Emma. With an icy expression, he stands before our masseuse and says something to the stranger, who is a whole head taller than him. Whatever Durand said, it makes the guy back off. I see him raise his hands in surrender and move away. But what I see next makes me want to throw up. Our little Canadian turns to Emma, wraps an arm around her shoulders, and signals for her to follow him. Just for the smile she gives him in return, I want to punch him. I discreetly follow the two to the VIP area. Once there, Durand proudly presents his companion to the other guys with a triumphant grin. Then, being the gentleman, he offers Emma a seat on the couch and sits beside her. As I approach the security guys, Parker seizes the opportunity and joins them. The other guys move closer, attempting to engage Emma in conversation. *She's like a light attracting all the moths*, I realize. None of them notice that I'm back. I take advantage of this and settle into one of the armchairs at the edge of the VIP area. From here, I can closely observe the guys and their conquest. They're acting like kids, competing for her attention. Parker pushes his martini on her to ensure she has a drink. Durand sits so close to her he could practically have her on his lap. And Toby... well, Toby is being Toby. Just our crazy Swiss guy. I have no idea what he just said, but the others are looking at him in disbelief. Only Emma laughs and clinks glasses with him. Emma. My gaze is glued onto her stunning face. She has accentuated her feline eyes with dark makeup and applied rouge to her high cheekbones, making them even more prominent. Thanks to Jess, I am familiar with women's makeup tricks. Not that it would have the same effect on her as it does on Emma. No, all the makeup in the world wouldn't be enough for that. But she knows how to bring out the best in herself with it. I push aside the subtle guilt that creeps in as I think of Jessica and continue to observe our masseuse. Deep within me, a desire awakens to trail my tongue along her neck, to taste her skin. As if trying to shake off these thoughts, I shake my head. *Damn it, Caleb, you have a girlfriend*, I remind myself. Although I try to avert my gaze from this tempting woman, I can't. It's like being magnetically drawn to her perfect body, tracing over her breasts, clearly outlined under the dress. The flat stomach, the hips, thighs, up to the point where her dress ends, revealing bare skin. I am surprised to spot the delicate lines of a tattoo. It runs along the back of her right thigh towards her buttocks. I can only see a portion of the tattoo, partly because Emma has crossed her legs. Upon closer inspection, I also discover a tattoo on her left leg. It's like a floral vine, ending just above the knee. I follow the intricate lines snaking down the outer side of her calf to her ankle. I can't make out the end, as Emma's feet are in white high heels. I am surprised because I didn't expect her to be tattooed. But damn, it makes the woman even hotter than she already is.

When I tear my gaze away from her legs and look up, I see that Emma has spotted me. While Parker talks beside her, she looks directly into my eyes. I can't say what is going through her mind, but one thing is certain: this woman is too tempting to resist. She holds my gaze, igniting a desire in me to dismantle Durand and all the other apes surrounding her within seconds. *Fuck! What is this? What is wrong with me?* Toby, following Emma's gaze, spots me too.

"Hey, Whyler!" he shouts at me. "What's up with you? Why are you just sitting there like you're waiting for someone to pick you up? Get your ass over here." It's only the empty cigarette pack he tosses at me that makes me avert my gaze from Emma's feline eyes. I swallow the heat in my throat and stand up.

"Make a little space for our buddy," Toby says, pushing the others aside. "You too, Durand, don't spread out wider than you are." With that, our goalkeeper grabs the Canadian by the arm and pulls him closer. Now, there is a spot right next to Emma. I see her smiling up at me, her fingers invitingly tapping the couch beside her. As if on autopilot, I sit down next to her, inhaling the floral perfume that wafts up my nose.

"Hi Caleb," she says with a sweet voice. "So nice to see you." Her hand, resting on my forearm and sending a fiery impulse towards my loins, is the final straw. That is enough! Who am I fooling here? I am not here for the game or for Parker. I never was. No, I am here because I want to meet Emma. Because I can't bear the thought of leaving her alone with Durand and the other idiots. I wanted to see her, wanted to make sure none of them got too close to her. Damned, cursed shit, I want this woman, I have to have her! *Fuck, fuck, FUCK!* I scream in my mind. This doesn't suit me at all. I am taken, I can't just ditch Jess. She'd go ballistic, create a huge fuss with her father. Who knows, maybe she'd even get him to kick me out of the team. I wouldn't put it past her to have that kind of influence on him. After all, she is his only child, his sunshine. I should get Emma out of my head and go home. Damn it, I'm twenty-seven, I can control my feelings! Just as I am about to muster the strength to get up, Parker stands up and waves over the VIP waitress.

"That was a damn great game today," he declares, hands on his hips. "Just three more wins and we're in the playoffs!" Toby and the others raise their fists in the air and cheer. "This calls for a celebration," Parker announces, turning to the approaching waitress. "Whiskey for everyone!" he shouts, prompting the players to cheer again. It is clear to me that I am not going anywhere.

9

EMMA

"Alright then!" Parker raises his whiskey, his gaze serious as it sweeps the room. "To our impenetrable defense." He nods in Byers' direction, then shifts the glass towards Toby, who sits with a broad grin, nodding. "To our goalies, the finest any team could wish for." The glass moves on, raised in Toby's direction, and I can't help but smile as all eyes turn to me. "To our sharpshooters." This praise extends to Caleb, Durand, and, as we all know, himself. "And to our new lucky charm. May you bring us many more goals." I smile sheepishly as all attention remains on me. "To the damn strongest hockey team in the world!" Parker concludes his toast, prompting all the players to raise their drinks and chorus, "To the Devils!" They then bring the glasses to their lips, downing the high-proof liquid in one go. Their drinking prowess leaves me astonished. Whiskey brings tears to my eyes just from the scent, yet they consume it as if it were water. It's no wonder Patrick couldn't keep up. Thank goodness I indulge in alcohol occasionally and can handle my liquor. Riley says I can hold my own for my size. Still, I resolve to take it easy tonight. After all, the tiny piece of pizza I had hardly provides a solid foundation.

Breaking the Ice

As Parker settles back beside me, I take a tentative sip of the amber liquid, aware of Caleb's gaze on me.

"What's up?" I ask, turning to face him.

"You should be careful with that stuff," he says, his expression making me chuckle.

"Why? Are you worried about me?" He doesn't answer, he just looks at me seriously. I'm about to wave it off, saying I have no intention of overdoing it, when Parker leans across me towards Caleb.

"Hey, buddy, someone wants to talk to you." He offers him his phone. Caleb furrows his brow as he reads the caller's name, his expression darkening.

"Damn. Excuse me, please," he grumbles, takes the phone, stands up, and heads over to the security.

"Oh, oh, I'm just saying, 'Thunder in Paradise'," Parker says, laughing.

"Thunder in Paradise?" I repeat, trying to figure out what he means by that.

"Yep, that was Jessica, his girl. She's pretty clingy and not a fan of him going out without her."

Right, Caleb's taken. With a handsome man like him, I can imagine his girlfriend isn't thrilled when he goes to a club without her. I watch him go, descending the steps and heading for the exit. *He wouldn't leave, would he?* A slight feeling of disappointment washes over me. *But that's silly, I'm not here because of him, I'm here to have fun.* Durand, who shifts closer to me again, distracts me from my thoughts.

"I must say that dress suits you perfectly. You look dangerously good," he murmurs in my ear, before giving me an appreciative once-over. I could return the compliment. In his white shirt, sleeves rolled up, and jeans, he looks really good. Actually, all the players have really dressed up today. I'm not used to seeing them like this.

"Hey, what's going on here?" I hear Parker ask, momentarily distracted because he was flagging down the waitress. Now he's leaning on his knee with one hand and throws Durand a frosty look over my head.

"You're interrupting, that's what's going on here. I have something to celebrate with Emma, so buzz off."

"Oh yeah? And what's that?"

"His tenth goal of the season," I reply.

"Pah, and he thinks that's a reason to celebrate? Well, Emma, you'll probably have to drink a lot tonight. Because this season, I've already scored fourteen goals." Parker clenches a fist and proudly points his thumb at his chest. And then, as if they both want to claim me, they move closer to me. I feel trapped, I can feel the heat from their bodies.

"So, Emma, what would you like to drink?" the Canadian inquires.

"You dimwit, she already has something." Parker gestures to the whiskey glass in my hand.

"Kid, you really don't understand women, do you?" Durand signals the approaching waitress that he'd like to order. Then he turns to me. "What'll it be, my beauty: champagne, wine, or perhaps a cocktail?"

"I'd actually prefer a glass of orange juice." My answer makes Parker burst into laughter.

"Yes, Durand, you're a real ladies' man," he teases him. But the Canadian remains undeterred, orders the OJ for me, and another whiskey for himself.

"I see you're tattooed," he says, as soon as he's placed the order. Durand's finger casually traces the spot on my knee where the flower vine tattoo ends. The touch is harmless, yet shamelessly sensual. It stirs a subtle ache in my lower abdomen, which I ignore, keeping my composure.

"Yes," I reply casually, "I'm into body art."

Breaking the Ice

"Alright, we have something in common then." With a sly half-smile, he watches me with his best flirtatious look. For the span of a heartbeat, I'm hypnotized by his eyes, reminiscent of melted chocolate. No doubt, this guy knows how to use his looks. I bet he's had dozens of girls falling for him with that face.

"How many tattoos do you have, if you don't mind me asking?" Parker redirects my attention to him. I see that his gaze rests on my left thigh, where beneath the hem of my dress, feather tips of a dreamcatcher are visible. The tattoo is one of my larger ones, covering three quarters of my left buttock and most of my thigh.

"A few," I reply evasively. He doesn't need to know how many tattoos I have.

"I bet you're pierced too, aren't you?" The gleam in Durand's eyes when he asks this is evident. He's hoping for a 'yes'. Well, I could tell him that I have two nipple piercings and three genital piercings - I removed the belly button ring because everyone and their cat has one - but I'll spare my breath. His mental cinema is probably running full throttle already. No need to feed him more information.

"Here come our drinks," I divert and smile at the waitress. As she provides us with orange juice and whiskey, I feel Durand getting restless beside me. From the corner of my eye, I see him lick his lips and gaze at my bare legs. I don't need to be a genius to know what's going on here. The Canadian is hot for me. While he might have found me appealing before, now he's got me in his sights for sure. Caleb's warning and request not to get involved with the players comes to mind. Maybe coming here wasn't such a good idea after all. *Nonsense, I just need to keep him at arm's length,* I decide.

"So, here's to your ten goals," I say, raising my orange juice and clinking it against Durand's glass. Before he can respond,

Breaking the Ice

I turn to Parker. "And to your fourteen goals." He grins, toasts with me, clearly thinking I'm engaging in conversation with him. But instead, I turn back to Toby. Luckily, he happens to be looking in my direction, and I manage to catch his gaze. "And to the best goalie!" I toast him and receive a joyful smile in return.

"Wait, wait!" I hear his voice muffled through the disco noise. "We need to toast properly." The red-haired giant stands up, comes over to me, squeezing himself between Durand and me. "Make some room, kid, I need to toast with the lucky charm," he grumbles at the Canadian. Judging by his expression, he's seething with anger, but he doesn't dare confront the Swiss. Annoyed, he turns away and joins Byers and the two girls sitting with him. "To the best goalie," I echo Parker's words from earlier and clink glasses with Toby. "Now, tell me, what brings a European to Portland?"

"The love for the sport, I'd say." While Toby shares his life story, I exhale and sink back into the couch. As sweet as my two admirers are overall, their intrusive behavior is starting to get to me. Parker is still sitting next to me, but he doesn't venture closer because every time he edges nearer, Toby gives him a warning look. I learn that our goalkeeper was born and raised in Switzerland, moved to London at 18, and played for a renowned hockey team there. Mr. Flake discovered him during one of his stays in England and recruited him directly for the Devils. With his size and deep voice, Toby can be intimidating to many. But once you get to know him, you realize he's a really nice guy. At least I do. He's like the big brother I never had. We talk for a while about his passion for hockey, and I let him convince me to try a Long Island Iced Tea. Eventually, we get onto the topic of women. To his regret, he's only had one serious relationship in his life.

"And you really only had one girlfriend?" I ask, raising an

77

eyebrow. It's hard for me to believe. After all, he's the most outspoken of them all.

"I'm not exactly proud of that," he says, scratching his neck in embarrassment. "At twenty-nine, that's pretty pathetic, isn't it?" Suddenly, I feel a deep sympathy for him. There's a pain on his face that hits me unexpectedly.

"May I ask why you haven't been with more women?"

Toby shrugs his broad shoulders. "I don't know, I find it hard to approach them." He looks at me, realizing that I don't quite understand what he's trying to say. He sighs and explains, "You know, when I'm with the guys, it's easy for me to make a stupid remark. But when I'm alone with a girl, then..."

I understand. "...You lack the safety of the group."

The goalie twitches his wide shoulders, indicating I hit the nail on the head. When he approaches a woman alone, he's vulnerable. And every rejection, every brush-off is directly aimed at him. *Despite being a mountain of a man, he's internally a wimp*, I think to myself, but keep my thoughts to myself.

"But right now you're also talking to a woman alone, to me."

"That's easy..." He waves it off, and before he finishes his sentence, I know what's coming. It's easy for him to talk to me because he doesn't want anything from me. "... you're not exactly my type". The words are barely out of his lips when he realizes what he's said, and his eyes widen in shock. "Oh, shit, that's not what I meant!"

"It's okay." I smile reassuringly.

"It's not because you're not good-looking. You're beautiful. But you probably already know that." His lips form that same embarrassed line again. "I just happen to really go for blonde women. Preferably with blue eyes and... a lot of wood in front of the hut."

"A lot of wood in front of the hut? I'm not familiar with

Breaking the Ice

that expression." Must be something European.

"Well, a good amount of this," he explains, raising both hands and indicating ample breasts.

"Oh, okay, got it." I suppress a smile because it looks funny how he's weighing non-existent breasts. "You know what, I'll help you," I say, placing a hand on his knee. Toby's gaze shifts first to my hand and then to my face. A furrow forms between his brows.

"Are you serious?" he asks in a noticeably softer tone, leaning down to me. He sounds skeptical.

"One hundred percent. You'll see, we'll find a great woman for you." The laughter that appears on his lips warms my heart.

"That's great! Oh, but one more thing."

"Yes?"

"Please don't tell the others that you're helping me. They'd tease me about it forever." I put my thumb and forefinger to my lips and mime zipping my mouth shut.

"Don't worry, I'll be as silent as a tomb."

"Good. Okay, where do we start? What should I do?" He sits up straight and rubs his hands together.

"Well, I know your type. Blonde, blue-eyed, and... What was it, a lot of wood in front of the hut?" He nods, grinning. "Well, for starters, I don't need to know anything else. Let's go dance."

"Dance?" His voice trembles.

"Yes, why not? It'll do you good to loosen up a bit." Toby's gaze jumps to his teammates. I understand he's embarrassed because all the others are up here watching him. Let's see if we can change that. I stand up, place my glass on the side table next to the chair where Caleb was sitting earlier, and turn to the players. Standing tall, one hand on my slightly tilted hip, I look at the men. "Alright, guys, I feel like dancing. How about it, who's joining me?" Parker, Durand, and Byers, whose date

Breaking the Ice

is appropriately miffed, rise immediately.

"Are you serious?!" I hear the petite brunette, here with the defender, screech. She crosses her arms over her chest, glaring up at him angrily. That's it for him. He slumps back into his seat, grumbling to himself. Poor guy, he's in for it tonight, I think. There's no need for jealousy, though. I might find Byers likable, but I don't think he's targeting me. After all, he's not hitting on me like the others. Shrugging in my thoughts, I turn my gaze to my new friend.

"Toby?" I say, extending a hand toward him.

"I'm not sure," he hesitates, but Durand comes to my rescue.

"None of that, big guy, you're coming." He grabs the Swiss man's arm and pulls him to his feet. I'm not sure if this is Durand's revenge for pushing him away from me earlier, or if he's trying to do me a favor. However, it works. Toby is actually persuaded to join us downstairs. This greatly lifts my already good mood, so as soon as I reach the mirrored surface, I raise my hands above my head and dance into the circle with small steps and swaying hips. When I turn around to face the others, I see them standing at the edge, watching me. At first, I don't understand what's going on with them. Then I notice the many shards of light casting onto my body from the dance floor. It looks incredibly beautiful, but it's definitely not the reason for their staring. No, it's my white dress, its fabric barely holding up against the light. Depending on how the specks of light hit me, my silhouette is visible. For a moment, I consider going back. But then I look at some of the women around me. Many of them have necklines where you can see down to their belly buttons. Others wear shorts with their buttocks hanging out, or dresses that barely cover their underwear. No, I definitely don't need to hide here. Besides, I love my body. And I'd be lying if I said that this doesn't turn me on in a certain way. So, I

Breaking the Ice

beckon the three of them to me with my index finger. Durand is the first to heed my call. Toby and Parker exchange an uncertain glance before they gather their courage and join us.

The DJ plays 'Bailar' by Deorro feat. Elvis Crespo, one of my favorite songs. Aside from Parker, who displays an outrageously good sense of rhythm, the other two stand like logs. I dance around them and encourage them to join in. At first, they hold back, only swaying their upper bodies slightly. But soon enough, I manage to sweep them along. Three songs later, the dance floor belongs to us. It's a blast with the guys. Although Parker and Durand try a few times to dance with me in a suggestive manner, I casually evade them and dance with Toby. The Swiss guy is a riot. I've never seen a man dance like him. It's hard to explain, but he reminds me of a duck. Arms bent and pressed against his chest, he sticks out his butt and sways it to the beat. It looks somehow cool and hilariously funny at the same time. Because the other two eventually get on my nerves with their attempts to dance provocatively, I grab the goalie and pull him onto the platform with me. I'm surprised that he follows me without objection. And, once we're on the platform, he rocks the house with his duck dance. He grabs one of the pole-dance poles and puts on a show that makes the people below us cheer and attracts a crowd of spectators. Some of them are filming his performance. I let loose as well, winding myself around the second pole and enjoying the evening.

At the end of the second song, I suddenly see Toby stumble next to me. From one moment to the next, he turns back into a log and stares down into the crowd. I follow his gaze and spot a blonde girl smiling up at him. With glowing cheeks, he desperately tries to find his way back to the beat. In vain. To spare him the embarrassment, I stop dancing, step to his side, and applaud him. The crowd follows my lead, turning Toby's

Breaking the Ice

cheeks tomato red. While the people cheer, we descend from the platform and return to Parker and Durand on the dance floor. I hold Toby back as he tries to escape and go back to the VIP area.

"Wait!" I call out to him over the music. Then I push him towards his friends, promise to be back in a moment, and search for the blonde girl. I find her with her friends at the bar across from the DJ. Without hesitation, I approach her and explain that Toby thinks she's super cool but is too shy to talk to her. The girl's name is Mandy, and she's clearly smitten with the Swiss guy. We exchange a few more words and agree that I'll stay with the guys on the dance floor while she sneaks up on him. Done deal. As soon as I'm back with the three players, the girls show up. While Mandy's friends occupy Parker and Durand, Toby's chosen one dances up to him. I grin when I see sparks flying between them. *That was easier than I thought.*

While everyone around me is having a good time, I savor the moment just for myself. I close my eyes, sway my body to the beat of the music. When I open them again, my heart skips a beat. Caleb stands at the edge of the dance floor, watching me. His hands are in his pockets, his gaze caresses my body. Now I feel like Toby earlier; I struggle to stay in rhythm. And then something happens that I never expected. He steps onto the dance floor and comes straight to me. A fiery thrill of excitement shoots through my chest. When Caleb stops right in front of me, I'm like a statue. He leans down to me - I can smell his spicy, rugged cologne.

"Would you give me this dance?" he asks, his words crackling in my ear. I feel his lips barely graze my earlobe, and I shiver. With a look that makes my legs go weak, Caleb straightens up again and extends his hand to me. Only now do I realize that the DJ has changed the music genre, playing a slow song. I place my fingers in his, sending a fiery impulse up my arm and making it hard for me to swallow. Caleb moves closer to me, guides my hands to the back of his neck. His proximity clouds my mind. I look up at him dazedly, wondering what's suddenly gotten into me. Maybe someone spiked my drink. The effect he has on me isn't normal! His hands, gently trailing down my sides and resting on my hips, erase any further thoughts. At this moment, I don't care if someone spiked my drink or if I just had too much to drink. Damn it, I don't even care that Caleb has a girlfriend. Here and now, I just want to savor this indescribably hot feeling that his closeness ignites in me. I want to be close to him, touch him, have him for ME. Even if it's just for this one dance.

10

CALEB

Even if I wanted to, I can't resist the allure of this woman. Emma is captivating, pulling me in like a magnet. I watched her from the bar for over half an hour, until I couldn't take it anymore and finally approached her. Now, as I dance with her, feeling her body against mine, it only intensifies things. I have to hold myself back from letting my hands wander over her incredible figure. She manages to make me hard just by being close. Her sweet perfume infiltrates my senses like an aphrodisiac. In a daze, I sway with her to the sounds of "Call Out My Name" by The Weeknd, feeling her hips move beneath my hands. I sense the stares of the other players on us, knowing that some of them don't like what they see. But I couldn't care less. The world could end right now, and I still wouldn't let go of Emma.

Three, four, maybe even five songs later, the DJ switches back to faster music. I can't say how many there were, I'm too intoxicated by this woman. Eventually, she pulls away from me, which feels awful. I'm already thinking that she's going to brush me off like the other guys on the team and send me away, but she doesn't. Instead, she cheekily smiles up at me

Breaking the Ice

and dances to one of those Latino songs. She puts a few steps between us, raises her hands above her head, and moves her hips in a way that could make a saint kneel. As if her sight wasn't already jaw-dropping, the fog machine behind her starts working. I can see white mist curling up around her calves. It looks like she's standing in a surging sea. My gaze follows her hands as they sweep down her sides from her breasts to her hips. My already hard cock twitches in response. Good Lord, what would I give for this woman to be mine? One thing's for sure, if this evening lasts much longer, I'm going to need an ice pack for my balls tomorrow.

It's half past three when I step into a taxi with Emma, and she gives the driver her address. I had to promise Toby that I'd make sure she gets home safely. He wanted to take care of her himself, but that would have meant sending away the little blonde who was hanging on his arm. Durand and Parker, both of whom had indulged a bit too much, of course, offered as well, but that was out of the question for both Emma and our Swiss friend. So, it came down to me, the only one who practically hadn't touched a drop of alcohol.

"Are you cold?" I ask when I see her rubbing her arms.

"No, I'm okay," she says. *Yeah, right*, I think to myself, holding back a smile. Emma is clearly more than a little tipsy. She seems a bit dazed, and her speech is slurred, something she's trying to hide. I slip out of my jacket and drape it over her shoulders.

"Thanks," she mumbles, pulling the fabric up to her chest. "I shouldn't have let myself be talked into that second Long Island Iced Tea," she confesses, tucking a strand of hair behind her ear.

I refrain from reminding her that I warned her. To be honest, I even took advantage of her state. Her rising alcohol level made her seek physical contact with me. Our last dance, damn, that was almost dry humping. Judging by Durand's and Parker's looks, they would have happily stabbed me on the spot. But I didn't care. Being so close to Emma was incredible. My cock was constantly hard, and I would have done, and still would do, anything to be able to take her home with me. I look at her, contemplatively studying her profile. This is the woman who should fall asleep next to me, not Jess. I want to wake up next to her beautiful face. Damn it, every day. I'd love to call Jessica and tell her to get out of my loft, where she's waiting for me. I lower my gaze to Emma's legs, where goosebumps are visible. An image comes alive in my mind. I see her lying naked in my bed, her tattooed legs wrapped around my lower back. My hands rest on her hips, pulling her up so I can thrust deep into her. I see her wonderful face, marked by pleasure. I hear her moan my name. Caleb, oh yes, Caleb!

"Caleb... Caleb!" Her voice snaps me out of my daydream. I lift my head from Emma's legs and look into her face. "Are you okay?" A brief blink dispels the impure thoughts.

"Yeah, of course."

"Okay, we're here. Thanks for coming along." It's only now that I realize we've stopped in front of a high-rise building. Emma is about to take off my jacket from her shoulders when I gently place my hands on hers, signaling her to stop.

"No," I say softly, "it's cold outside, keep it on." Then I turn to the taxi driver. "Would you please wait a moment? I want to accompany the young lady to the door."

"Sure thing." The middle-aged man turns off the engine and turns on the radio.

"After you," I say with a deep gaze into her eyes. I see her lips part slightly. She considers saying something but decides against it and steps out. As she does, her dress rides up a bit, giving me a glimpse of the curve of her hips. Fuck! I have to clench my teeth to resist the urge to raise my hand and touch

Breaking the Ice

her.

Shutting the car door behind me, I follow Emma, walking along the sidewalk next to her towards the building. The outdoor lights flicker on as we ascend the five steps to the entrance. While she digs in her purse for the key, I lean against the wall next to her and watch. In my chest, that overwhelming desire to take her with me comes alive again. I don't want the evening to end, I don't want to just let her go. The bright jingle of her keychain, which she retrieves from her bag, triggers a feeling of helplessness in me. She can't leave yet! Not now, not before I've tasted her lips. Before I realize what I'm doing, I take a step towards her. Almost on its own, my hands cup her face. For a heartbeat, I lose myself in the brown of her eyes. Then I lean down to her and steal a hungry kiss. Emma's lips are soft and warm. They seem innocent, but then I feel her mouth open. Her tongue requests entry, which I grant her with an excited groan. My cock presses painfully against my jeans as she lifts her hands and wraps them around my neck, her tongue stroking over mine. This woman tastes incredible, to say the least, divine even, and she's driving me out of my mind. With my body, I press her against the glass entrance door, letting her feel how horny she's making me. Emma's perfect body is trapped beneath me, which turns me on even more.

"You're driving me crazy; do you know that?" I growl into her mouth. My words make her shudder. Her fingers dig into my hair. She lifts one leg, wraps it around my thigh, and lets me press my hardness against her. The heat emanating from her most intimate place makes my cock throb. I bet she's soaking wet. Just the thought of it sends my testosterone into overdrive. I slide my hands to her ass, wanting to grab and lift her, when the light in the hallway behind her comes on. Dazed, I let go of her as the realization of what I've just done slowly seeps into my mind. Emma sways a little, prompting me to support her by the upper arm. *Fuck, you're such an asshole, Whyler*, I shout at myself in my thoughts. *The girl is drunk, and you, you horny bastard, shamelessly take advantage of the situation – and what about Jess?*

"I'm sorry," I say, watching as she looks up at me in confusion, adjusting her dress. The expression on her face cuts straight to my heart. *She deserves better than a cheating piece of shit like you*, a malicious voice in my head hisses. Before Emma can respond, the door behind her opens, and a heavily made-up young woman steps out. "Well, then," I say remorsefully, "see you on Monday." With that, I turn away, leaving behind the most incredible woman I've ever met, and walk away.

My jaw aches as the taxi driver drops me off in front of my loft. Throughout the ride, I've been wrestling with my guilty conscience, teeth clenched. I should tell Toby what I did with his new friend, he'd probably punch me. That's exactly what I deserve. Someone should beat the shit out of me. Damn it, how could I let myself go like that? I shouldn't have gone out; I should've stayed in and had a cozy evening at home with Jess instead. Jessica, I bitterly contemplate. I know she's waiting for me in my bed upstairs. *The wrong woman - she's the wrong woman*, hisses the voice in my head. As if I don't know that myself!

Taking two steps at a time, I ascend the stairs to my apartment. A tremendous anger boils in my stomach. I'd love to smash everything to pieces. Starting with myself. I slam the apartment door shut behind me, then head to the kitchen and grab a beer from the fridge. *As if that would be enough*, I think, put it back, and retrieve the Scotch from the bar in the living room. I skip the glass and take a hefty swig straight from the bottle. The alcohol burns in my throat, but I don't mind. Let it dissolve me from the inside out, for all I care.

"Hey babe, there you are. I was getting worried," I hear Jessica's voice. I don't need to turn around to know she's standing on the stairs leading up to my bedroom. "Did you have a nice evening?" The question makes me exhale in frustration. *A nice evening? Damn right I could've had a nice evening! A damn nice one, if it weren't for you*, I growl inwardly. Another sip of Scotch washes down the bitter taste on my tongue.

"Caleb?" Jessica's hand rests on my shoulder from behind. "Darling, what's wrong?" *What could possibly be wrong? I'm trapped in a nightmare, that's what's wrong. I'm with a woman I want nothing to do with anymore, just because her father could kick me off the team if I leave her.* It's the first time I openly admit to myself that I don't want Jessica anymore. To be honest, I never really did.

"Everything's okay," I lie. Putting on a casual expression, I turn to face her. Jess's blue eyes look at me lovingly.

"Come to bed," she says, takes my hand, and leads me behind her. It feels wrong to go upstairs with her. Even the two more swigs of Scotch I take don't help. When we reach the bedroom, Jess takes the bottle from me and places it on the floor. With a seductive look, she pulls me into bed with her. She wants to be fucked. It's her way of dealing with jealousy and testing my loyalty. She knows me, knows that I need a break after sex before I can get it up again. So, if I don't get hard now, she assumes I cheated on her.

"Can't we postpone this to tomorrow?" I ask while she pushes me onto my back and starts unbuttoning my shirt. "I'm really dead tired." Jessica ignores my words and leaves a trail of kisses from my left nipple - which she bites into - down to the waistband of my jeans. "Jess, seriously. Let's do this tomorrow..." Too late, her skilled hands have already freed my cock and are playing with it.

"I'm pretty sure he's not tired," she purrs, taking my tip into her mouth and sucking on it. Fuck. I close my eyes and see Emma's face in front of me. I lick my lips, trying to remember her taste. "Well, I knew it," Jess rejoices because I'm getting hard. If she only knew it's not her blowjob skills but the memory of Emma that's pumping blood to my lower region, she'd rip my balls off. "Mhm," she moans, working her way down my length. She's making an effort to please me, but I can't disconnect. Even though I've been walking around with a constant hard-on all evening, now, with Jessica crouched between my legs, sucking on my cock, the desire fades. I try to pull myself together, to think of Emma, how I pressed her against the front door and kissed her. Or her sensational ass, which I caught a glimpse of when she got out of the taxi. But it's all in vain. This feels wrong, and accordingly, my body responds. I feel my cock deflate. My diminishing arousal speeds up Jessica's movements. She scratches my balls with frantic fingers, massaging my shaft.

"Sorry, but this won't work. I had too much to drink," I say as Jess sits up and looks at me accusingly. For a tiny moment, she seems to consider. Then she swallows the lie and grins at me. Damn, she gave me a blowjob; now she expects me - if I can't fuck her - to reciprocate in some other way. But everything in me rebels against going down on her. So, I sit up, grab her arm, and pull her with her back against my chest. Now she's sitting in front of me with her legs spread. She realizes what I intend to do and slips out of her panties. I just want to get this over with. So, I reach past her, slide two fingers of my left hand into her slick pussy, and massage her clit with the other. Jessica writhes against my chest and moans lustfully. I block out how she starts to sweat beneath me, eagerly pressing her center against my hands. In my mind, I'm far away, with a woman whose taste has indelibly etched itself into my memory. And then Jessica's voice, hoarsely gasping my name, brings me back to the present. She climaxes on my hand. I feel her pleasure running down my fingers. Not long ago, this would have turned me on. Today, I'd prefer to wash my hands right away.

"That was... wow, just wonderful!" she raves breathlessly. She turns her head and plants a kiss on my neck before getting up and heading for the stairs. "Are you coming?"

"Go ahead. I just need to put this back," I explain, pointing at the bottle of Scotch. "As you wish. But don't take too long. I'll be waiting for you," she says with a wink. "Oh, and Caleb..." That sounds more serious.

"Yes?" I raise my gaze and look at her.

"I love you." Oh...

"The orgasm did someone some good, huh? Go shower now, you little minx," I deflect, playfully throwing a sock at her. I can't possibly find the words to say it back. Luckily, she doesn't notice that I'm changing the subject. She giggles, throws the sock back, and goes down the stairs. I exhale and collapse back onto the bed. What a load of crap. I feel like absolute dirt. What I just did was beyond low. It's not fair to Jessica. Sure, I'm not into her anymore, but that's still no reason for my shitty behavior. Can a woman you hardly know really turn your world upside down so much that you turn into an asshole overnight? I mean, I'm not usually such a scumbag. Restless from guilt, I sit up and run my hands through my hair. Then I think of Emma, who just an hour ago had her fingers tangled in my curls. Again, I lick my lips, hoping to taste a remnant of her. "This is madness," I murmur to myself. No matter how much I want this woman, I have no intention of alienating Jessica and risking my career with the Devils. So, I'll have to get Emma out of my head. Whether I like it or not.

11

EMMA

Breathless and with a pounding heart, I slowly open my eyes. I've just had a rather wild lewd dream.

I was at the Brillant, swaying on the dance floor to the beats of Shakira's 'Chantaje'. There was no one there but me, except for Caleb, who stood in the shadows, observing me. I couldn't see him, but I could feel his presence. White mist crept up my legs. I knew I couldn't stop dancing, and I knew Caleb was controlling the mist. Guiding it up, under my dress. It felt exquisite, caressing my intimacy and brushing like a cool tongue over my pearl. I could feel Caleb's gaze on me. He watched as my hands, filled with mounting desire, moved to my breasts, caressing myself. Embracing the white mist between my legs, I surrendered to the ecstasy he bestowed upon me. Soon, he drove me towards climax. I sighed, closed my lids, and moaned as I came. With goosebumps covering my legs, wherever the mist touched me, I finally opened my eyes again.

Now, I wasn't alone anymore. Toby, Durand, Parker, and all the other lads from the team stood at the edge of the dance floor, gazing at me with expressionless faces. I knew they had been watching me. The feeling of being observed was as arousing as it was unsettling, ultimately waking me up with a fiery throb between my legs.

As the images of my dream slowly fade, I blink up at the ceiling. My drenched underwear reminds me of last night. What the hell did I do that got me so aroused?

I focus on the time at the club, but my memory only spits out individual sequences: the pole dance with Toby, Durand, and Parker, who were hitting on me from both sides, and the Long Island Iced Tea. I think I had a second one. Or did I? Yes, Durand talked me into it.

Another fragment of memory pushes through. Toby met a girl. Mandy, a petite blonde. There was quite a spark between them. I feel a bit uneasy, so I sit up, and am immediately met with a sharp pain in my temple.

"Damn it," I groan and reach a hand to the sore spot. It then occurs to me that I'm wearing a jacket. "What on earth...?" I throw back the sheet and look down at myself. Beneath the unfamiliar top, I'm still in the shoulder-less white dress from last night. Man, I must have been pretty out of it not to manage taking it off.

On an impulse, I cast a glance back at the bed. I'm alone. Well, at least there's that! But whose jacket is this, and why the hell am I wearing it? Damned Long Island! I have no idea how strong the bartenders at the Brillant mix their drinks, but one thing's for sure: I'm never ordering one there again. I feel utterly wrecked. Out of curiosity, I take a sniff of the unfamiliar piece of clothing. Oh. That scent, that sensually masculine fragrance, I'd recognize it among thousands. Caleb – it's his jacket. A wave of heat washes over me, and I remember dancing with him. But that still doesn't explain why I'm wearing his jacket. I rummage through my memories, but it brings me nothing but more headaches. *Alright,* I think, *I give up. We definitely didn't have sex, because Dad would've personally thrown any guy out. Including Caleb.*

Hoping to feel a bit better afterwards, I force myself to get up and head for the shower. Unfortunately, all the warm water in the world doesn't help me get back on my feet. Although my stomach feels queasy, I decide to eat something. Maybe it'll help. I'm just glancing into the fridge when Dad appears in the kitchen doorway.

"Hey, feeling any better?" He looks concerned, hands on hips, bushy brows knitted together. How does he know about my hangover? I look at him, puzzled, and reach for a bottle of water. "Did you have to throw up again?" Wait, what?

"I threw up?" I ask incredulously.

"Yes, four times. Don't tell me you don't remember," Dad replies. My expression must speak volumes, as Dad's face shifts from worried to angry. "Emma!" he scolds, coming in and leaning on the table opposite me with his fists. "What on earth were you thinking? God only knows what could've happened to you! A pretty girl, drunk in a strange city. Good Lord, I can't even imagine what could've befallen you!" His voice reverberates in my head, almost causing him to explode. I squint my eyes shut and feel for the chair to sit down. Dad sighs resignedly. "How much did you drink yesterday?"

"Not much," I reply, rubbing my temples.

"But you don't look like you only had one or two drinks." *And I certainly don't feel like I did,* I think, taking a sip of water. Maybe it'll help.

"I'm telling you, Dad. I only had two Long Island Iced Teas." *You can't really count that tiny sip of whiskey.* "Normally, I can handle two cocktails, but yesterday I hardly ate anything for dinner."

"Well, there you have it! I've been saying, you're reckless." His fists thunder on the table. What's wrong with him? Why is he being so harsh? "And I told you to eat more. But no, little

Breaking the Ice

Missy here doesn't have to listen to her old man. You should've had something substantial in your stomach before leaving the house. Not that cardboardy slice of pizza. Besides..." The thought of something edible doesn't sit well with my stomach. I feel nausea rising. Shit! Right in the middle of Dad's lecture, I shoot up and sprint to the bathroom. I barely manage to reach the toilet before I vomit up the water I just drank. I retch dryly a couple of times before my stomach realizes there's nothing more to expel. Exhausted, I crouch over the bowl. I feel like a zombie – half-dead.

"Feeling okay?" I hear Dad behind me.

"I feel really terrible," I confess.

"Alright, come here. Up you go." His hands slide under my armpits. He helps me to my feet and guides me into the living room, where he settles me into his chair. Then he goes wordlessly into the bedroom, fetches my blanket and pillow, and sets up a makeshift sickbed for me on the couch. I feel like when I was a child. When I felt unwell during the day, I was always allowed to lie in the living room. That way, my parents could keep a better eye on me, and I didn't have to be alone upstairs.

"Thanks, Dad," I say as he helps me onto the couch and tucks me in. I'm extremely cold, so I pull the blanket up to my chin.

"That's alright. Just do me a favor and drink less next time, alright?"

"Don't worry, I won't touch alcohol for ages." *Or maybe never again.* Considering my condition, I think that's the more sensible option.

"Now, just rest up." He still seems angry, which I can't blame him for. While Dad settles into his chair and watches a sports show, I vegetate until my eyes eventually droop shut. When I wake up again, it's already late afternoon. Again, I feel somewhat okay initially, but as soon as I'm on my feet and I have some chamomile tea, it comes right back up. My circulation is in the pits. I constantly switch between shivering and hot flashes. In the evening, Dad makes me one of those packet soups. For his sake, I take two spoonsful, which are returned directly. It's not until the next morning that I feel better. I'm still a bit wobbly on my feet, but I manage to keep down my coffee and even dare a bite of bagel. Around ten o'clock, I get ready for work. Dad is against me going to the ice rink today. He says I should stay home and recover. But that's out of the question for me. I definitely don't want to sit around here and waste away. Plus, I want to know what's new with Toby, and I need to give Caleb's jacket back. The thought of the forward gives me a strange feeling in my stomach. Hopefully, I didn't embarrass myself in my stupor. After a lot of hassle, I manage to convince my father to take me. In my online schedule, where the players can sign up, there are only two massages. Parker at eleven and Toby at twelve.

At the ice rink, I head straight to my massage room. Promptly at eleven, Parker shows up. He's in a great mood and raves about Saturday night. If you were to believe his words, the guys have never partied so hard as they did with me. While he talks about Mandy's friends who couldn't get enough of him and Durand, I remember a dark-skinned girl. She clearly had her eye on Parker. I bet he took her home and had a hot night with her. That would certainly explain his good mood. Toby, who doesn't show up until twenty past twelve, is on cloud nine. He's head over heels. With a perpetual grin, he tells me about Mandy. She spent the entire weekend with him and completely captivated him. I'm happy that things worked out for them, and I make a mental note to interrogate Mandy a bit the next time I see her, to find out if she's serious about the goalie.

Breaking the Ice

After the two massages, I'm pretty beat. I actually want to go home and lie down, but Dad isn't finished yet. So, I use the time to look for Caleb and return his jacket. My first stop is the weight room. But it's deserted, and on the ice, I only find Durand and a few of the defensemen working on their stick skills. I'm sure Caleb is somewhere around because Parker was supposed to lift weights with him. So, I head to the locker room. Just like last time, a misty cloud greets me as I enter. The front area with the lockers and benches is empty. However, I hear voices coming from the hallway that leads to the showers. I bite my lip because I'm tempted to go back there. A few naked hockey player butts would probably be a nice sight. But that's definitely not an option. Maybe I should just leave the jacket here. My gaze lands on one of the rows of lockers. As far as I can tell, they don't have name tags. It's hard to say which one belongs to Caleb.

"Emma, what are you doing here?" a voice that pierces my defense startles me. Caleb comes through the hallway towards me with a towel around his hips and a bottle of shower gel in his hand. *Wow! Okay, girl, get yourself together. You know the guy is ridiculously well-built. You've seen him half-naked plenty of times.* But why does he stir up this nervous flutter in my chest? I lick my lips. There's something in my memories that's trying to surface. Because I don't want to stand there and stare at him like an idiot, I focus on giving an answer.

"I'm here to return your jacket," I say, watching as he, without taking his eyes off me, goes to the third locker from the left. He opens it and puts the shower gel inside. Then he comes over to me and stands about two steps in front of me with his arms crossed.

"Hey, Emma," Byers greets me from behind the forward, emerging and going to the right side to his locker. "Hey, party animal, have you recovered from the weekend? You sure had a

Breaking the Ice

blast, huh?" the defenseman remarks.

"Yeah, it was a great night, wasn't it?" I reply, hoping I didn't embarrass myself.

"Hell yeah! That calls for a repeat."

I force a smile and nod before turning back to Caleb.

"So, feeling better?" he asks quietly, so Byers can't overhear.

"Better?"

"Well, you weren't in great shape when I brought you home on Saturday."

"You brought me home?"

"Yeah, don't you remember?"

"No," I confess meekly, rubbing my forehead embarrassedly with my hand. "I probably shouldn't have had that second Long Island." How embarrassing. Of all people, Caleb has to find out about my blackout.

"You still look pretty rough. Quite pale. It's better for you to go home and lie down," the concerned tone his voice takes on when he says this touches me. I feel like he wants to raise his hand and stroke my cheek. But he doesn't. Instead, he just looks at me with a sad expression.

"All right, I was just about to..." I interrupt myself because in the corner of my eye, I see Byers dropping his towel. Now he's standing stark naked, not five feet away from us. I have absolutely no problem with naked men, but I might have one if Thornton catches me in here. He wouldn't appreciate me ignoring his guys' privacy. "I should go," I say hastily. "Here." I'm about to take a step forward to hand Caleb his jacket when he steps forward and wraps his arms around my lower back. Before I realize what he's doing, he lifts me up and to the side.

"What...," I stammer, pressed against his muscular chest.

"That was close," he says, casting a furtive glance at Byers, who's just getting a pair of shorts from the locker. Caleb gestures at the Devils logo emblazoned on the floor next to us. "You almost stepped on the logo," he explains, lowering his gaze to me. His intensely focused gaze that shoots straight between my legs.

"And?" I ask, a little dazed.

"That would've been bad luck."

"Bad luck?" I repeat, managing to raise an eyebrow.

"Yeah, the guys are pretty superstitious about that."

"Oh, only about that?" I tease him, becoming more and more aware of his proximity by the second. I feel his firm body, his warm bare skin under my hands. I wish I could explore his muscles with my fingers.

"Well, what can I say, hockey players are just superstitious," he replies, with an expression that sends a shiver down my spine. I swallow, currently unable to respond.

"Whoa, what's going on here?" I hear Byers ask. His amused tone makes me realize that I'm still in the arms of the forward. He must have seen me ogling Caleb. Damn! Feeling a bit embarrassed, I release myself from the embrace and take a step back.

"Okay, so I better get going," I explain, avoiding their gazes. "See you." With that, I turn around and make my exit.

12

CALEB

"My, my, looks like someone's got it bad for you, eh?" Byers remarks as soon as the door slams shut behind Emma. I don't answer, but I return to my locker with a grin I can't suppress. Yeah, I have to admit Byers is right, it seems our masseuse has taken a liking to me. I like it, a lot. The way she looked at me with those cat-like eyes... Fuck, how can you not get turned on by looks like that? Under different circumstances, I would've kissed her right here and now - slipped my tongue into her mouth. The memory of her fantastic taste has almost faded. I'll admit, I would've liked to taste her again. But I can't. Emma and I, it's an illusion I can't indulge in any longer. The fact that she doesn't remember the events of Saturday night, or more precisely, what happened outside her apartment, is my saving grace. That way, I don't have to worry about her telling anyone. I suppress the slight pang of disappointment I feel because she's forgotten our kiss. I know it's better this way.

Over the next two weeks, I deliberately keep my distance from Emma. I don't know how I'd react if she got as close to me as she did in the locker room. It's better not to take any risks, so I'll stay distant. But I watch her from afar, observe how Durand and Parker never tire of courting her. It sickens me. Those two are like herpes; you just can't get rid of them. Emma seems to get along really well with Toby and his new girlfriend, Mindy or Mandy - I have no idea what her name is. The three of them hang out regularly. Often, half the team joins them when they go out. I've noticed that the camaraderie among the players has improved since Emma arrived. We were already a tight-knit bunch, but now that the guys are doing things together more often, the bonds between some have become even stronger. This is also affecting their hockey performance. We were stronger than ever at the game last Sunday. Even Coach Thornton raved about it. And from Carl, the big boss, we each got a $500 bonus. The atmosphere at the Portland Devils, whether it's players or management, couldn't be better. That eases my mind because I couldn't stand more people with bad moods around me. Things are going badly between Jess and me. The last time we had sex was after the night at Brillant. Since then, every time she wants me, I make up an excuse. She senses that something's not right - accordingly, she's insecure and moody. It's annoying, but I can't change it. I just can't bring myself to touch her. Something in me resists. Maybe it's my guilt towards her, or maybe it's the fact that I can't stop thinking about Emma. It's frustrating. The more I try to get her out of my head, the more she haunts my thoughts. I tell myself it's only because I can't have her. After all, everything forbidden in life has a special allure.

Two weeks before Christmas, the whole team is eagerly looking forward to our next game. That game could lead us to the playoffs. Since in the New American Hockey League we play in, there aren't as many teams as in the bigger leagues, our regular season ends in January, while for others, it usually runs until late March or early April. Anyway, we're optimistic about making it to the playoffs and we train hard every day for it. When I come into the rink on Monday morning, four days before the big game, I find a note in my locker.

Meet me tonight at nine in the VIP area of the ice rink. And, Caleb, not a word to anyone!
T.

T? Who could that be? Toby, Thornton, or Terry, the guy from the souvenir shop? These note-passing games bother me. If any of them wants something from me, they should come out and say it. I crumple the note and toss it back in the locker. My mood today is downright dismal. Jess spent the morning bawling her eyes out because I turned her down again. Dealing with her is becoming a proper chore. To blow off some steam, I hit the gym hard. Afterward, I let Maxwell work out the knots. I'll give it to him, he's the best sports masseur we've ever had. Yet every time I lie on that table, I wish I were in the next room with Emma. Once, I caught myself holding my breath, listening, thinking I heard her voice. Knowing that Parker and Durand are still running their bet gnaws at me. Someone needs to clue Emma in. I'm even more convinced of this when I find out at afternoon practice that she recently agreed to go on dates with both of them. She went to the movies with Parker and Durand took her to some fancy restaurant.

"This day's been a right washout," I grumble to myself as I step into the shower afterward. I hear Parker in the locker next to mine, cheerfully whistling away. I'd love to shove the soap down his throat. And Durand, that smug asshole; someone ought to wipe that superior grin off his face. A wave of anger courses through my veins, making me slam my fist against the tile wall. I can't recall ever feeling so helpless. Emma doesn't deserve to be part of this damned bet. I wonder why Toby, her oh-so-good friend, doesn't set her straight. Why does he let

Breaking the Ice

this whole mess continue? Toby... the note in my locker springs back to mind. Suddenly, I'm burning with curiosity about who it's from. I decide to go and find out. If it's actually from Toby, I'll bring up the Emma situation with him. Since I'm not keen on experiencing another fresh Jessica drama, I kill the hour and a half at the rink. Grab some grub and exchange a few words with Terry, who's sprucing up his souvenir shop for the next game. I can confirm, the message isn't from him. He's in a rush, it's his wife's birthday, and he's taking her out.

At nine sharp, I find myself in the VIP area. I'm clearly not the only one who got a note. The entire team is here, save a few exceptions. Toby announces that he's the brains behind this gathering and motions for silence. I join him and cast a glance down at the empty ice below.

"What's all this then?" I ask, and the Swiss lad clamps his mitt over my mouth.

"Ssh, don't ruin it. We've got to be dead quiet," he hisses, his snowy brows knitted tight. "Alright, everyone come closer. But for God's sake, keep it hushed." He beckons the others up to the glass barrier at chest height. The VIP area is like a raised terrace, giving us the perfect view of the ice. Then Toby whips out his phone and dials a number. "We're ready. Let the show begin," he whispers, and all the lights in the arena go out. It's pitch-black for a moment until a blinding spotlight carves through the darkness. It zeroes in on the player's bench, where a woman in a beige winter coat and a white bobble hat steps out. It's Emma. She's wearing skates and glides onto the middle of the ice, followed by the beam of light. There, she stops and waits.

"What's she doing?" I whisper to the goalie.

"Just wait," he replies with a grin, aiming his phone camera at our masseuse and hitting record. I furrow my brow, gazing back down at the ice, and spot a figure approaching Emma.

Breaking the Ice

It's Durand. His face still wears that bloody smug expression. Emma lets him kiss her on the cheek, and it boils my blood. Just as I'm about to ask Toby what the hell this is and if the idiot is proposing to her, a second figure appears. It's Parker.

"Now, you all need to be dead quiet and watch closely," the goalie breathes to us.

"What's this about, what's he doing here?" we hear Durand ask. But Emma ignores the Canadian, lets my mate give her a peck on the cheek, and hands each of them a hand. Now Parker says something, but unfortunately, we can't make it out, he's too soft-spoken.

"Both of you are truly unique men," Emma declares loudly enough for us up here to hear clearly. Her gaze goes from Parker to Durand and back again. I'm too far away to read my two teammates' expressions, but I don't need to, their body language gives away their uncertainty. "No one has gone to such lengths for me," Emma continues, "and honestly, at first, I felt almost honored. Two handsome men like you, refusing to take no for an answer because you're so determined to win me over."

"You mean one handsome man. But yes, a woman like you only comes along once in a lifetime. That's why you should fight for her," Durand gushes.

Yet Emma doesn't engage with him this time either, but continues, "As I said; initially I felt honored…" Fuck, I'm beginning to grasp what's going on here. "…Until four days ago when I brought Durand his phone in the locker room, which he had forgotten after the massage with me."

"My phone… four days ago?" The confusion in the Canadian's voice is audible even up here.

"Yes, Durand, four days ago. When you two were chatting in detail about your little bet in the shower." *She knows!* I bite my lip as an indescribable feeling of joy spreads in my chest.

Breaking the Ice

"No idea what you're talking about," Parker responds, agitated.

"Oh really? Well, you two bet on who could bed me first. If Durand loses, he gets his flow and eyebrows shaved off before the final. If you lose, Durand gets to fire three pucks at you. Tough luck for both of you because you've both lost. Neither of you will get me." *How damn amazing is this woman?* I cheer in my mind. Now I understand why she went out with both of them. She wanted to give them the feeling of being close to their goal. Probably to ensure this trap here worked and they both showed up. Durand, the wannabe, was still strutting around in the locker room today. He boasted in front of the guys about how close he was to the goal and how Emma was already eating out of his hand. *So much for that*, I think, grinning devilishly. She gave that asshole a lesson he won't forget anytime soon. *Good on her!*

"Alright, listen, you know what..." Parker raises both hands in surrender. "...Let's just call it quits, alright? You caught us and won."

"Parker's right, you clever thing, you've seen through us. Let's leave it at that. It doesn't help anyone if we spill the beans to the others." *Well, look at that, suddenly Mr. Bigshot Durand isn't so cool and laid-back anymore, is he?*

"Well, I wouldn't put it like that. There's definitely one person it helps. And that's me. You've played me, treated me like a toy." I see Emma plant her hands on her hips. "I think your punishments are absolutely fitting. It's only fair that you receive them. Lost is lost."

"Too bad for you, you have no evidence whatsoever, do you? Parker and I will deny that you found out. We'll just say Toby told you about the bet. That makes it null and void." Durand looms threateningly over Emma, trying to intimidate her. *He's a pig!* "Come on, Parker, let's get out of here." He's about to turn away when this brave little woman on the ice grabs him by his Devils jacket and holds him back.

"Just a moment," she says with a firm voice. "I figured you'd react like this. So, I took precautions. Byers!" As soon as she calls the name of the defender, a metallic click echoes in the arena, and a second spotlight switches on. It's directed at the VIP area and thus at us players. The guys around me erupt into deafening cheers and applause for Emma. Blinded by the spotlight, I can barely make out the expressions of the three on the ice. But from what I can see, Durand and Parker lose all color from their faces, while Emma grins broadly. The phone in my pocket vibrates. I pull it out and see that Toby has shared the incriminating video in our WhatsApp group. Now even those who missed the show can see how our sweet masseuse put two men in their place.

"Just when I thought I was mad at you for not telling Emma about the bet," I say to Toby, who gives Emma a thumbs up.

"I wrestled with it for a while," he confesses, turning to me. "After all, these bets are a matter of honor. But when I finally wanted to clue her in, she already knew."

"Wasn't she angry with you? After all, you're kind of like her best friend here."

"Oh, she was! If Mandy hadn't explained to her the value of the bets for us men and that I was forced to keep quiet, she probably wouldn't have forgiven me until today." I smile as I watch Durand and Parker slink off the ice. "But she did. She's a fantastic woman."

She certainly is, I confirm in my thoughts. *And more than that.*

13

EMMA

"Oh, I think it's about to start!" Mandy shouts beside me, struggling to contain her excitement in her seat. I look down at the ice, where the Devils' mascot is doing its rounds. Loud music reverberates through the arena, while a projector displays the best goals and plays of the home team onto the ice. Today is the big day, the guys are facing off against the Salem Flyers. If they win this game, they're guaranteed a spot in the playoffs. I watch the colorful spotlights sweep over the rows of spectators. It's unbelievable how many people are here. If I understood Dad correctly, the game is completely sold out. The commentator's voice rings out, announcing the home team, as the music continues to swell, sending the fans' blood boiling. They're already pounding their giant drum and starting a chant. I love the last few minutes before the game starts. They're always so charged with emotion. And then, it's time. The players of the Portland Devils shoot out of their bench one after the other like arrows, sending the crowd into a frenzy.

"Yeahhh, go Devils!" my friend shouts, jumping up and applauding the guys. I follow suit, seeing the players' glances sweep up to us - checking if their lucky charm is present.

Breaking the Ice

Only the two wingers - Parker with number 8 and Durand with number 10 - ignore me. They skate their warm-up laps in the upper half of the field with their heads down. Although it's been four days since I embarrassed them in front of their teammates, they're still angry with me, which; admittedly, I couldn't care less about. Let's be honest, the two of them deserve it. Making bets at the expense of others is just shitty. You just don't do that. They brought this on themselves, so now they have to deal with it.

"And here he is, the man from Two Rivers. Our top scorer with the magic stick. Sixty-seven goals in this season alone! Welcome our man for all occasions, the forward star of all forwards, CALEB..." echoes the announcer's voice through the arena, and all Devils fans, including us, respond with full-throated, "WHYLER!" And then Caleb, number 19 with the captain's badge on his chest, shoots out of the bench and the arena erupts. The Devils' fans drum is pounding in my ears. It plays a drum roll until Caleb has completed a show lap and knocks down the puck pyramid in front of Toby's goal with a prepared puck. Then everyone cheers again, and Toby with player number 1 takes his place. I see him looking up at us and blowing Mandy an air kiss. Then he turns to his second love, Samantha, his goal. He tenderly strokes her frame, and if I'm not mistaken, he's moving his lips. He's probably talking to her again.

"Toby's relationship with that goal is pretty crazy," Mandy says beside me, shaking her head. "He's so superstitious and thinks that if he doesn't honor Samantha, or treats her badly, they'll lose."

"He's not the only one in the team who's superstitious, believe me," I say, looking at Caleb, who's doing his laps. I love watching him on the ice. His movements are so smooth and powerful at the same time. The announcer's voice rings out

Breaking the Ice

again, welcoming the guests, the Salem Flyers. At the same time, the JumboTron, hanging high above the center of the ice, displays the Flyers' logo on its four screens. It's a blue wing that ends in an S for Salem. I compare the blue and white jerseys of the opponents with our red and black ones and believe that our guys look much better.

At last, it begins. The teams take their positions, the referee drops the puck, and the players surge forward. It's an insane game. The Devils are in their prime, making the Flyers look outclassed within minutes. The first line, composed of the wingers, or forwards as they're known, Parker and Durand, along with the center, the crowd's favorite, Caleb, is the strongest. They're outrageously good, scoring an incredible four goals in the first period and entertaining their spectators royally. Mandy beside me is even more invested than I am. She keeps jumping up from her seat, shouting: Foul! High stick! or Hooking! The referee hands out a few penalty minutes to both teams because the guys are overdoing it with their body checks. By the end of the second period, it's clear that the Flyers have lost. They're trailing with zero to six goals and are helpless against the determination of the Devils.

When the final whistle finally blares through the arena, both the fans and the players are ecstatic. The guys skip their massages because they just want to celebrate their victory. *Works for me, I'll be done early today*, I think as I head home. Dad stays back at the ice rink. He's planning to catch a ride with Bill later. The two of them have been spending quite a lot of time together lately, which I find unusual. My father is usually a typical couch potato and prefers to spend his free time at home in front of the TV. On one hand, I'm glad he and Thornton get along so well. On the other hand, I find his sudden urge to go out strange. Still, I don't bring it up with him. He must know what he's doing.

Breaking the Ice

Arriving at the apartment, I receive a WhatsApp message. It's from the Devils group. A new, unfamiliar number writes:
⋆*Tonight, big playoff entry celebration at Caleb's Loft! You're all invited!*
⋆Toby: *Hell yeah, we're definitely coming! Start chilling the Jägermeister!*
⋆Byers: *Count me in!*
⋆Durand: *I'm bringing a date.*
Oh, Durand's bringing a girl? Good for him, I think. Let's hope he doesn't ruin it with some stupid bet. Shaking my head, I head into the bathroom and run a bath. While I enjoy the bubble bath, I call Riley. She can't wait to see me again in two days. I'm going to spend the Christmas break at home in Aberdeen and I'm really looking forward to it. Even though I love Portland and my job here, I miss my friends and Mom. While Riley and I chat, WhatsApp messages keep coming in. I don't check them, I'm sure it's the players confirming their attendance at Caleb's party. As for me, I plan to have a quiet evening. Pizza and an old horror movie, maybe. Let's see what Netflix has to offer.

An hour later, the water isn't even lukewarm anymore, so I end the call and step out of the bath with wrinkled hands. Wrapped in my bathrobe with a towel turban, I'm about to head to my bedroom when the doorbell rings. *That must be Dad. He's probably forgotten his keys*, I assume, and open the door.

"Emma! Why aren't you answering my messages?" Mandy snaps at me, rushing past me into the apartment. "I'm completely beside myself," she whines.

"What's going on?", I ask, closing the door behind her and ushering her into the kitchen.

"Well, it's about tonight. About that stupid cow, Belinda."

"Belinda?" I repeat, my forehead creasing. "Should I know

this woman?"

"Yes! Well, no, I think she was before your time. I mean, before you started with the Devils. She's Toby's ex-girlfriend." I understand. She's that one girlfriend he had. Still, I don't quite grasp what Mandy is getting at.

"And?" I inquire.

"And she looks super hot, still seems to want him according to the texts I saw, and she's coming to the playoff party tonight with Durand!" The words are just pouring out of my friend. She's completely worked up, with red stress spots on her face and neck. "Emma, I know you had planned a quiet evening tonight. But I need your support. I don't want to face that cow alone. Please, come with me to the party."

"I'm not sure..." After the embarrassing incident in the locker room when Caleb lifted me off the logo and I gazed at him like a lunatic, I've been steering clear of him. I've realized he's got me all tangled up, and it's healthier to avoid him. At a party in his loft, I'm bound to run into him.

"Emma, please. This really matters to me. I need you." Mandy takes my hand, looking at me with her baby blue eyes, pleading. Man, how can you say no to that? Well, I'll just accompany her. No one says I have to hang out with Caleb just because I'm in his loft. I'll just stick close to Toby and Mandy.

"Alright then," I agree, after which Mandy throws her arms around my neck.

"You're the best, Emma. I owe you one," she says, letting go of me. "Okay, so we'll pick you up around half past eight. Can you make it?" I glance at the digital clock on the stove. That's in just under an hour.

"Yeah, I should be able to make it."

"Perfect! I'm looking forward to it, it's going to be great! God, I have to go, get all dolled up." Fidgeting like a startled chicken, Mandy heads toward the door. "Thanks again! You're the greatest! See you later!" And off she goes. *Crazy thing*, I think with a smile, and head to my bedroom to rummage through my clothes. *What on earth does one wear to a playoff party in a loft?*

At half past eight, I stand in front of the mirror in my wardrobe and look at myself. I've opted for skin-tight jeans that accentuate my butt, and a loosely falling glossy black top. I'm wearing black high heels and silver hoop earrings, which make my neck look so elegantly long. I've tied my hair into a high ponytail today, and my makeup is understated. Just some eyeliner to accentuate my eyes, a bit of mascara, blush, and done. I grab my handbag and head downstairs. Outside the house, I look around for Mandy, who seems to be running late. So, I take the opportunity to call Dad and let him know I'm going out. But my father's phone is turned off, which is unusual for him. I leave him a message and I'm just considering calling my friend to check up on her when Toby's SUV pulls up. They're running late because Mandy couldn't decide what to wear. Now she's in a pink balloon dress that makes her look like a giant piece of candy. Not exactly an outfit I'd have chosen. But she has to feel comfortable in it, not me. On the way to the party, my friend chatters non-stop. She's insecure about this Belinda, but Toby takes it easy. I see him place his massive hand on Mandy's slender thigh, soothing her. The two of them are so sweet. I wish I had someone who could calm me like that. I don't know why, but the thought of meeting Caleb is making my heart race. Nervous bubbles churn in my stomach, and I wonder if I'd have been better off staying home.

We arrive at one of those old factory buildings on the outskirts of town. Whoever renovated this place is a genius. Although it looks ultramodern on one hand, it hasn't lost its original 1920s flair. The front has a cigar shop, Old Habana. Through the tall windows and glass door, I can catch a glimpse

Breaking the Ice

of an elegant dark wood interior and hefty wingback chairs. Toby leads us past the closed shop to a door at the side of the building leading to Caleb's apartment. Even in the stairwell, we can hear voices and music. Again, discomfort bubbles up in me. *I shouldn't have let myself be talked into this*; I lament silently. Too late, I can't back out now, because Toby is opening the door to Caleb's loft.

"Alright, folks!" he calls out, drawing everyone's attention. "Your Swiss fun guarantor is here. Let's get this damn awesome party started! Woo-hoo!" *Oh man, classic Toby.* I enter the apartment with Mandy and can only gape in astonishment. I never would have expected Caleb to have such taste. The loft is insane! Almost everything is in white. The walls, the curtains, the kitchen, even the floor. It's made of one of those new poured materials. On the left side, there's a black leather couch in front of a built-in massive screen and an extravagant glass table with black claw feet. On the walls hang carefully chosen black and white watercolors, and on the right side, next to the XL kitchen, I spot a black iron staircase leading to the upper area. The apartment is filled with people. It looks like the whole team is here. I think I even saw Mr. Flake, and I wonder if my dad is here too. Toby hooks Mandy and me under his arms and leads us to the couch, where Byers and Parker are sitting. I join the winger, who doesn't seem too thrilled and turns away from me. His stubborn behavior is starting to get on my nerves.

"Honestly, are you still mad?" I ask bluntly. For a moment, I think he's ignoring me, but then he sighs and turns to face me. The gaze of his ice-blue eyes roams over my face. I can see the hard expression around his lips disappear, replaced by a regretful smile.

"No, it's just..."

"Just what? Just that you lost your bet and can expect a few bruises? Sorry, my friend, but you brought this on yourself."

"I didn't want this to happen." A wistful look comes into Parker's eyes. And there's something else, a deeper emotion... Oh no. "Emma," he continues, taking my hand in his, "the bet was a huge mistake. When you started with us, you were just the pretty new girl that everyone wanted. I didn't think much of it to bet for one night with you. But then I got to know you and..." *No, please don't say it!...* "I fell in love with you." *Damn it! Why didn't I listen to my gut feeling, you stupid nut? I should've stayed home!* "I've never met a woman like you before. You're so different, so..."

"Parker, wait," I interrupt him before he can go any further. He pauses and looks at me with hopeful, raised eyebrows. Oh damn, I hate moments like these. "Listen, you're really a good guy, but there will never be anything between us." My radical honesty causes his shoulders to slump.

"It's because of that damn bet, isn't it?" *No, it's because you're just not my type,* I think, but I nod and let him believe it's because of the bet. That's less painful. "Ah, damn it, I knew it. I screwed it up myself, I am an idiot." Parker lets go of my hand and runs his hand over his closely cropped hair. "Is there anything I can do? Make it right?" He tries to reach for my hand again, but I pull it back and shake my head regretfully. "Ah shit," he curses and stands up. Looking down at me, he seems to consider whether he should say something else but decides against it and walks away. Phew. I exhale. I hate having these conversations.

"Emma, look, there she is. Belinda," Mandy whispers urgently in my ear. She didn't catch the conversation between Parker and me because she was distracted by the couple at the other end of the room, who are now making their way towards us. Durand and a girl in her mid-twenties. She has waist-length blonde hair, a generic face, and a regular figure.

Breaking the Ice

She towers over the Canadian by half a head and overall seems pleasant. That changes when she spots my friend.

"Seems like someone isn't exactly a fan," I whisper back to Mandy, never taking my eyes off Belinda.

"The feeling's mutual," my friend hisses.

The two haven't reached us yet when Toby appears behind them.

"Durand, where have you been lurking that you dragged this rat here?" he inquires with a stern expression, squeezing past his colleague and the girl. He brings us our drinks. I'm totally stunned that the usually friendly and always joking Toby would say something so offensive.

"Have a nice evening, Toby," Belinda retorts with a dreadful high-pitched voice. "You don't seem to have changed at all."

"Oh, I've changed alright. I've learned to recognize dirt clumps from true gems." With these words, he sits down next to Mandy and puts an arm around her shoulders. The air between them is thick. I wonder why Durand brought the girl here. He must have known that Toby isn't fond of her. And suddenly it dawns on me that he's seeking revenge on him this way. After all, Toby helped me expose him and Parker. *What an asshole.* I lean over to my friend.

"Sweetie," I whisper in her ear, "this woman is no threat to you. She couldn't hold a candle to you in a million years."

"That's become abundantly clear to me too," she replies with a relieved smile. Whatever Belinda messed up; Toby wouldn't touch her with a ten-foot pole anymore.

"I need to make a quick visit to the little girls' room. Can you manage on your own?"

"Of course, go ahead," she answers, still keeping her eyes on her rival. I stand up and walk through the revelers towards the back, where I assume the bathroom is. I admit I don't actually need to use the bathroom, I just wanted to escape the tense atmosphere. Tired from the long day, I lean my back against the staircase railing leading to the upper floor and take a sip of my soda. I watch some defenders engrossed in their animated conversation. Further back, I see Parker, staring out the window, drowning his disappointment in an amber-colored drink – whiskey, I suspect. Seeing him stirs up a twinge of guilt in me, so I peel myself off the staircase and continue to wander through the crowd of guests. Standing next to a floor lamp with a black shade, I observe the couch from a safe distance. Belinda is now a bit further away, her back turned to Toby. Great, it seems like things have settled down. Just as I think the coast is clear and I can go back, my scalp starts to tingle.

"What interesting thing are we looking at?" a voice inquires directly in my ear, causing my heart to stumble in shock. It's Caleb; he's standing close behind me, his handsome face only inches away from my ear. I turn to face him and see him straighten up, amused, in his white shirt and low-slung jeans. His hands are behind his back as he looks at me expectantly. Oh man, of all people, he catches me spying on my friends.

"Caleb, hi. Great party," I try to deflect, but he's not easily distracted.

"Come on, spill. Who were you watching?" There's open curiosity in his eyes. "Durand?" Interesting. There's a tone of disapproval in his voice, as if it bothers him that I am snooping on him.

"No, not Durand. Just the girl he's here with," I say, waiting eagerly for his reaction.

"Belinda?" His nostril twitches as he quirks a corner of his mouth.

"You don't seem to like her very much," I observe.

"No wonder, nobody likes her. She squeezed Toby dry,

blew all his money, and then, when he was broke, moved on to the next one." Caleb looks at her with contempt. "You should've seen him back then. After the relationship with that money-grubbing hag, he was down in the dumps for weeks."

"Heard she never quite gave him up and still texts him today."

"Let her," Caleb shrugs. "She's lost Toby for good." He averts his gaze from Belinda and looks at me. "Let's drop this unpleasant subject." He pauses briefly, during which his eyes narrow by a fraction. He seems to be considering. "Is everything okay with you?" he asks. Ah, so that's the issue. I inwardly sigh, knowing where he's heading.

"If you think I'm bummed about the bet, you'll be disappointed." I knew it! Judging by Caleb's expression, I hit the nail on the head. "Granted, I wasn't exactly thrilled about it, but I got my revenge."

"Yeah, you did, and I have to admit, you did it quite well." With these words, a smile lights up his lips, making my knees go weak. *Man, this guy just looks outrageously good.* "You're taking this whole thing quite lightly, aren't you?"

"Probably because I wasn't interested in either of them," I try to prevent myself from looking at him, but as I say it, I lose myself for a moment in Caleb's eyes. Somewhere inside me, the desire to raise my hand and touch him awakens. There's something between us, a kind of flutter.

"Is there someone you are interested in?" Caleb's voice sounds different, rough. His gaze darkens. I believe he feels this vibration between us too. Without taking his eyes off me, he slowly, like a predator, takes a step towards me. "Who is it that you want?" he murmurs. Now I'm sure, he feels this crackle, this magnetic pull between us. His proximity makes me forget all my resolutions to stay away from him and not do anything stupid. I want to tell him that I want him. That it's him I desire – more than anything in the world. I open my mouth, take a deep breath to say what's on my mind. Caleb's eyes travel down to my lips. The moment passes as if on fast forward. But just as I make a sound, a woman's voice drowns me out.

"Oh, Caleb, who do we have here? Aren't you going to introduce us?" I blink in surprise. A blonde girl hangs onto the forwards' arm from one moment to the next and smiles at me artificially. Caleb steps back a few inches from me and swallows hard.

"I... so... this is Jessica Flake... my girlfriend," he stammers. Obviously, he's just as taken aback as I am.

"Nice to meet you. I'm Emma, the new masseuse," I introduce myself and shake her hand. Jessica's brain takes a second to process. Then her expression changes in an instant. It's like a mirror shattering. And now all the shards – in her case, all the friendliness – come crashing down, leaving behind pure aversion in Jessica's case.

"This is the new masseuse?" Hand on her hip, she snaps at Caleb. "You didn't mention a word about her looking like a fucking Miss World."

"Jess..." he starts, but she doesn't let him get a word in.

"No, none of that 'Jess'! I can't believe the crap that's going on here. How dare Thornton hire her?" Suddenly, a look crosses her face that sends a shiver down my spine. "Now I know why you've only been at training lately. You're fooling around with this little tramp. Aren't you?!" *Excuse me? Did she just call me a tramp?*

"Are you completely losing it?" Caleb shakes off her hand, which is still on his arm. "You better apologize to..."

"To who? This little whore?! For sleeping with my boyfriend?!" Her voice escalates at the last word, and something inside me snaps. Without weighing the consequences, I raise my hand and pour the rest of my soda in her face. It makes her gasp for air. "You disgusting little slit-eyed bitch," she curses at me, but by then, I've already turned my back on her and walk past the guests who have stopped their conversations, back to my friends. "You'll pay for this!" the blonde screeches behind me. Back when I was a young girl, I might have turned around and slapped her, just so she has a reason to act this way. But today, I'm wiser and won't engage in such nonsense.

"Can you guys give me a ride home?" I ask Toby and Mandy, who are already about ten steps ahead of the couch. They both sit there with open mouths, staring alternately at me and the cow. I don't wait for their answer, I just say, "I'll be waiting downstairs." Then I leave the loft under the gaze of the attendees and go down the stairs. *Why, Emma? Why don't you listen to your gut?* I scold myself in my thoughts. *I shouldn't have come here in the first place. This is all just one huge mess!*

As I arrive on the ground floor and open the front door, I hear someone upstairs leaving the apartment. *Thank God; at least Mandy and Toby aren't leaving me behind,* I think, and step out into the cool night. Wrapping my arms around my upper body, I walk along the gravel path and around the building. I'm barely around the corner when I hear the front door open with a click, followed by the crunching of gravel. *That must be Mandy. She's such a darling,* I think, and turn around to face her.

"Don't worry, I'm perfectly fine," I lie. But instead of my friend, I recognize Caleb coming around the corner towards me. Oh, I hadn't expected him. "You've got a sweet girlfriend there," I say sarcastically. But he doesn't respond to my words. Instead, he comes closer in long strides and pushes me against the glass door of the shop. It tickles a memory buried deep in my subconscious – one that refuses to surface.

"Emma..." His hands pressed against the glass on either

side of me, he holds me captive. "What did you want to say earlier?" Oh my God, his gaze is so intense, I feel like I'm incinerating under it.

"What do you mean?" I ask with a trembling voice. His closeness claims me, calms and unsettles me at the same time.

"You know what I mean. I want to hear what you wanted to answer me earlier. Who is it that you want?" I swallow, seeing his dark gaze roam over my face.

"You know the answer," I whisper. I'm not capable of more.

"I want to hear it." He leans down lower towards me, his warm breath brushing against me. "I need to hear it. Tell me, who do you want?" he implores me. I blink against the tornado of emotions raging inside me. Uncertainty, hope, affection, desire...

Then, a single word escapes my lips: "You."

14

CALEB

"Emma!" Toby and Mandy's shouts shatter the moment. They rush around the corner to their friend's aid. When they spot me, they slow down and come to a halt.

"Caleb?" Toby looks at me with a furrowed brow. I raise a hand to signal him that we're not finished here yet. Then I turn to Emma, who looks back at me with uncertainty, sandwiched between her friends.

"This is what I wanted to hear," I say gently, wanting to cup her face in my hands and kiss her, when she lets out a regretful sigh.

"Unfortunately, that doesn't count."

I move closer to her, sensing that something has changed.

"What do you mean?" A nauseating feeling of foreboding creeps over me.

"Caleb, you should go back to Jessica."

"Why are you saying this?"

"Because I can't do this. I'm sorry, but I can't bear to stand between you two." I hear the painful tone in her voice, see the suffering look in her eyes.

"This problem can be fixed. I'll leave her here and now."

It's the only right thing to do. I don't care if she then runs to her daddy and tries to turn him against me. I've crossed that line definitively. Determined, I push myself off the glass, ready to go upstairs and end the Jessica Flake chapter, when Emma stops me by the arm.

"Wait, Caleb! That wouldn't change anything. You would have left her because of me because I pushed myself into your relationship. I don't want that... I can't do that." Emma's last words are no more than a whisper. I see a telltale glint in her eyes. "I'm sorry," she whispers, stands on tiptoes, and plants a kiss on my cheek. Then she leaves me, head bowed.

"Emma!" I call after her. "Please don't do this, don't go!" Desperation courses through my veins, hot and scorching. Toby and Mandy, following their friend, give me a sympathetic look. I run my hands through my hair, not knowing what to do to salvage the situation.

When I eventually hear the car doors of Toby's SUV slam shut and they drive away from the parking lot, a fuse blows in me. "Goddamn it!" I shout, kicking the trash can in front of the Old Habana out of sheer anger. The force of the blow yanks it out of its anchoring, causing it to crash down with a dull thud. Its contents – a few coffee cups, cans, and other junk – spill out onto the gravel.

"Fuck," I growl, pacing back and forth in front of the store. Following Emma is pointless. But I also don't want to go back to the party. I don't know how I'll react if I see Jessica's face again tonight. She called Emma a slit-eyed whore. That damn bitch! No, I can't possibly go back upstairs. Let them enjoy the playoff party without me. I need to get out of here.

Fishing the key to my bike out of my pocket, I head downstairs to the garage to retrieve my racing bike. There's only one thing that will help now: alcohol.

★★★

Breaking the Ice

"Hey Baby, there you are again," a concerned voice pierces through the fog in my head as I try to lift my eyelids.

"Is he awake?" That's another, much deeper voice. Slowly, I come to, which feels like emerging from a deep mire. I blink against the veils in front of my eyes. The image sharpens, and I recognize Jess and Parker. They're standing next to me, by a bed... a hospital bed – in which I'm lying!

"Am I dead?" I ask because that's exactly how I feel.

"Doesn't look like it, but it wouldn't have taken much more," my buddy explains, shaking his head down at me. "What were you thinking?"

"Thinking about what?" I ask, sitting up, which makes my already pounding head feel like it's about to explode.

"Caleb, yesterday morning we found you a block away from the Brillant. You had an accident." The Brillant? Yes, of course, I got wasted there. And then there was this girl dancing on the pole who reminded me of Emma. I wanted to see her, talk to her. So, I got on my bike and... after that, I don't remember anything.

"Wait a minute! Did you say yesterday? How long was I out?"

"Nearly 36 hours," Parker explains, making Jess sob beside him.

"I was so worried about you," she whimpers, stroking my shoulder.

"Jess, I..."

"No," she interrupts me. "Don't say anything. I don't know what got into you that night or what was going on. But I want us to put it behind us." She tries to smile, stirring up the guilt in me once again. *I have to end this, I have to tell her that I don't feel anything for her anymore.* I'm just gathering the courage, about to be honest with her, when there's a knock on the door.

Toby appears. He sticks his head inside the door and grins

when he sees that I'm awake.

"Well, who's this rising from the dead?" he exclaims with delight, entering the room with Mandy in tow.

"I'll go get some coffee then," Jessica announces, a hint of annoyance on her lips. She can't stand the two of them. That doesn't surprise me, after all, they're on Emma's side.

"Alcohol poisoning, motorcycle accident... Whyler, I'd say you really went overboard. You were damn lucky to walk away from that crash with just a few scrapes," the Swiss guy remarks, clicking his tongue in reproach and pulling up a chair. "But now tell me, what's it like to have your stomach pumped? Does it hurt?"

After my closest friends visit me, Coach Thornton, Byers, and some of the other players drop by. The coach gives me a good chewing out for my recklessness and drills into me that a professional athlete doesn't behave like this. As if I didn't already know.

I have to stay for two more days for observation, giving me plenty of time to think. First and foremost, it's clear to me that I will definitely break up with Jessica. It's over between us. And if her father really decides to kick me off the team just because I dumped her, well, go ahead. Let him try to find a center as good as me. Besides, I'm confident I can find another place to go if needed. I can't be with a woman I don't love for the rest of my life just to secure my position on the team.

I've learned from Mandy that Emma is gone. She went to Aberdeen for the Christmas holidays and won't be back until New Year's Day. Until then, I have enough time to sort everything out here. Christmas is the most wonderful time of the year for Jessica. I don't want to ruin the holiday for her, which is why I've decided to wait until after the festivities. It will still be tough for her when I break up with her, but at least she won't be drowning in tears on her beloved Christmas.

Breaking the Ice

On December 22nd, the opening of the art exhibition that Jess has been preparing for weeks finally arrives. She's incredibly nervous, getting her hair, nails, and who knows what else done to look perfect. I'm annoyed that I have to go, so I persuade Parker to accompany me. At 8:00 PM, the exhibition is formally opened by Professor Weinstein in the foyer of the art museum. Jessica's father has spared no expense or effort to secure the best location for his darling. While Jess talks to potential buyers, Parker and I stroll through the exhibition. None of the paintings speak to me; on the contrary, they bore me. Just like everything here.

"Is everything okay with you?" I feel Parker's gaze on me and meet his eyes.

"Of course, why do you ask?"

"I don't know, you've been acting a bit different lately. You seem introspective, unhappy." That hits the nail on the head. Knowing that Emma is in Aberdeen and that I won't see her before New Year's is tearing me apart. I want to sort things out between us, convince her that she belongs by my side.

"I have a lot on my mind right now."

"It's because of Emma, isn't it?" I don't want to answer that, not before I've ended things with Jess. "I knew it, it's because of Emma." Of course, Parker interprets my silence correctly. "Well, I can understand that. She's a unique woman. Make sure you don't make the same mistake I did and lose her," he says, his mouth forming a sad line.

"I don't intend to," I say seriously, turning to the next painting. My gaze falls on the double doors at the entrance, through which Durand has just entered. What does he want here? I watch him suspiciously as he looks around, spots Carl and his wife, and approaches them with a broad smile.

"What's going on?" Parker must have noticed my furrowed brow. He turns around and follows my gaze. "Why is the

Canadian here?"

"Good question. Looks like he's here to butter up," I say, wrinkling my nose in distaste, as I watch him kiss Jessica's mother's hand. Then he turns his attention to the boss and engages him in conversation.

"That bastard," my buddy growls. "You do realize he's after your spot, right?"

"My spot - what do you mean?"

"He wants to dethrone you. Durand thinks he's the better forward."

I laugh humorlessly. "That's ridiculous."

"It is. But not in his eyes. I've been watching him cozy up to Thornton and Mr. Flake for a while now. At first, I thought it was about me that he wanted to replace me as an assistant. But then I overheard him on the phone, saying that the fans will be chanting his name during the entrance next season." Now, that's news.

"And why are you telling me this just now?"

Parker shrugs. "I told you; you've been acting weird lately. I didn't want to add this bullshit on top of it."

I nod and put a hand on his shoulder.

"You know what? Let's get out of here. I've seen enough brown-nosers and bad art for today."

"But we haven't even been here for half an hour."

"I don't care. I'm fed up. Let's go play pool."

"Pool sounds good. Let's get out of here." I don't even try to fight my way through to Jess, who is still occupied by guests. Instead, I send her a text message:

I'm out, see you later.

Then we make our exit. Parker and I are descending the few steps in front of the brick building when the double doors behind us swing open.

"What's going on here? You're not really making a run for

it, are you?" Durand stands at the top of the staircase, a smug grin on his face.

"Get lost," I say, but the Canadian doesn't back off. He walks alongside us and positions himself in front of me at the foot of the stairs.

"Are you deaf or something? I told you to get lost," Parker hisses. I can see a muscle in his cheek twitching with anger. Durand remains unfazed, sporting nothing but a mocking grin.

"Poor Jess will be pretty sad when she finds out you've bolted."

"I didn't bolt," I reply, unfazed.

"Oh, so you just got tired of her art then? You really have no clue about women."

That earns him a scoff from me. "You think so? Well, as far as I know, I have a girlfriend, while you recently got shown up by our masseuse." I know Emma is a sore spot for him, and it's evident in his expression. "Now get out of my way." With that, I shove him aside with the back of my arm and continue walking with Parker. I can hear Durand emit a contemptuous snort behind us.

"Don't try to play the big shot, Whyler. You'd have gotten shot down just the same by Emma. No one lands that arrogant witch. She doesn't even spread her legs with candy. But hey, you think you're something special, right?"

Candy? I abruptly stop in my tracks. "Whyler, ignore the jerk. Let's go," Parker urges. But it's too late, all alarms are blaring inside me. Candy – I'm sure that's the Canadian term for drugs. The evening at the Brillant comes to mind when Emma seemed so out of it. I swallow hard, force myself to stay calm as I turn to face him.

"What did you just say?"

"I said that you think you're something special." Durand

Breaking the Ice

struts towards me with swaggering steps. "But let me tell you something, you're not. You..."

"What did you mean by candy?" His furrowed brow shows he has no clue what I'm getting at. "Durand, did you give Emma drugs?" A volcano is about to erupt inside me.

"What?"

"Answer Whyler's question! Did you give Emma drugs?" In the corner of my eye, I see Parker step up beside me. Now he seems to have grasped the situation as well.

"And what if I did? Man, loosen up, you prudes. I just slipped the little one half a pill in her Long Island. A bit of good mood, that's all. What's the big deal? I had a bet to win, after all." Durand doesn't see my fist coming. He's completely unprepared when it hits him on his damn face. I feel his hard jaw beneath my knuckles, hear it crack. My right is followed by my left, burying itself in his stomach and eliciting a choked squeak from him. Durand's legs give way, folding him like a wet sack.

This miserable piece of shit deserves it! I'm going to finish him!

Parker's voice reaches my ears as if from a distant place. He's calling my name, but I don't care. This bastard here drugged Emma! I lean down to him, claw my fingers into his white polo shirt, ready to deliver the next blow. But before my fist can thunder into his face, I'm yanked back. Slim arms wrap around my upper body from behind, holding me back. I struggle, having only one desire: to beat the shit out of Durand.

"Caleb, calm down. Caleb, damn it!" Parker is trying to soothe me from behind. "Come on, buddy. Stop it, pull yourself together."

For someone so slender, he's surprisingly strong. He manages to hold me back enough for Durand to scramble to his feet and put some distance between us.

Breaking the Ice

"You goddamn asshole!" I scream at him, ready to throw myself at Durand again, when a voice makes me pause.

"Caleb!" It's Jess. "For heaven's sake, what is going on here?" The horror in her voice makes me calm down. "Caleb, I need to know what's happening!" she urges, as I don't respond but instead glare at Durand with a look full of hatred.

"It's alright. I just gave this loser a beating," I explain quietly.

"Pah, loser," Durand taunts and spits blood beside him onto the pavement. "I only see one loser here. And that's you, Whyler." His hand points up at Jess, who stands at the entrance, while his hateful gaze remains fixed on me. "You can't even be honest with your girlfriend. Playing like you love her, while you chase after Emma."

"The masseuse?" Jessica's voice sounds panicked.

"That's right, isn't it? The slut completely twisted your mind, didn't she?" As he calls Emma a slut, I try to free myself from Parker's arms once more.

"You're digging your own grave here," my buddy warns, to which Durand only spits on the ground again.

"Caleb, please tell me this isn't true. You don't want anything to do with that Asian girl, right?" I lift my gaze to my girlfriend, who comes down the stairs with tears in her eyes. *That's it, this farce ends here and now*, I think.

"No," I reply, breaking free from Parker. He seems to understand that Durand is my last concern right now and that I won't touch him again. "It's not true that I chased after Emma," I say, turning to Jess. "However, it's true that I want something from her. And I have for a while now."

"No..." She brings her hands to her mouth. I can see her blinking back tears.

"It's over between us," I say, to make this short and painless.

Breaking the Ice

"No, please," she whispers with a choked voice and reaches out her hand to me. I catch it with mine and look at her seriously.

"I'm sorry, Jessica. I never wanted to hurt you." Now the dam breaks and she sobs helplessly.

"Well done, asshole," Parker snaps at Durand. The Canadian's response is a raised middle finger.

"You can't do this to me, Caleb, please!" Jess throws herself into my arms and clings to me tightly. Damn it, I knew there would be a scene when I left her. The museum door swings open again. This time it's Professor Weinstein. I signal to Parker that we need to get out of here. We have to leave before the entire society, including my boss, witnesses this ugly scene.

In the Lucky Saloon, a billiards club, Parker and I find some peace. My phone has rung about twenty times in the ten-minute drive here, so I've turned it off. Although I had vowed never to drink alcohol again, I wash down the taste of adrenaline that still lingers on my tongue with beer. I tell Parker how unhappy I've been in this relationship for so long that I only didn't break up with Jess because I was afraid she might tarnish my reputation with Carl. Which, as you can see, I've managed just fine on my own. But I don't want to dwell on that now. We talk about Durand for a while. He's always been an asshole, but after Emma embarrassed him in front of the team, it's like he's dropped his facade. Now he's showing his true colors once and for all. At some point, we talk about Emma, and I confess that I've been blown away by her from the first day, that it's been hard for me to stay away from her. As I talk about her, I become increasingly aware of how painfully I miss her. And then I realize that I have to have this woman. Come what may. I won't wait for her to return, and I won't accept a 'no'! While I'm sitting with Parker in the Lucky

Breaking the Ice

Saloon, I turn my phone back on and send her a text message:
*I've left Jessica.

And then I write in a separate message:

*Emma, the only woman in this world that I want is you. I won't accept your 'no' any longer. You belong to me, and you know it.

15

EMMA

"Tell me, how was it at Riley's last night?" my mom asks at the breakfast table, a cup of green tea in her hands.

"Good, it was cozy as always. We were a nice small group."

"And was that football player there too? Lester?"

"His name is Jester, and yes, he was there." Jester is the kicker for the Washington Sharks and my ex-boyfriend - if you can even call him that. We were together for a few weeks this summer. Until I found out he had a little fling on the side because I didn't give it up right away. He said I got him so hot and bothered that he just had to relieve some pressure somewhere else. Idiot. I gave him the boot that very day. Since then, he's been trying to win me back at every opportunity.

"I find him nice and good-looking," Mom comments.

"And he's anything but faithful," I say, seeing a shadow pass over her face.

"Oh, that's certainly unpleasant," she says, getting up and going to the kitchenette. While she pours herself fresh tea, I look at her. With her silky black hair and slender figure, you could easily mistake her for me from behind, even though she's currently much thinner than I am. She's lost quite a bit of weight. Her jeans are practically hanging off her legs. I wonder if she's eating less because she's sad. It must be hard for her to suddenly be living alone in Aberdeen. She must miss Dad and me.

"How is it for you without us?" I ask, and she turns to me with a pained expression on her face.

"I'd be lying if I said it was easy," she says, lips twisting into a wistful smile.

"But you're managing fine without Dad and me, right?"

"Of course. Emma, dear, you shouldn't worry about me. I'm doing well." That doesn't sound sincere. Mom hides her face behind her big teacup, taking a sip. Then she comes over to me and sits back down at the table. Looking down at the newspaper next to her, she casually asks, "How's your father, by the way?" The question confuses me. I mean, they must talk regularly on the phone. Right? I think about it, but I can't remember overhearing a conversation between them. Something about this seems odd.

"He's doing well," I reply, watching her face closely. It doesn't show any reaction.

"And he really couldn't come home for the holidays?"

There! A hint of sadness crosses her face.

"No, as I said, he couldn't. Coach Thornton insisted that one of us stay present and available for the team over Christmas."

"Tzzz, Bill," she mutters with disdain in her voice. That's enough, something isn't right.

"Okay, Mom, what's going on here?"

"What do you mean?"

"Don't play dumb. I want to know what's happening between Dad and you. Are you fighting?"

"Fighting? No, everything is fine between us."

Oh yeah? Then why do I see tears welling up in her eyes? I

Breaking the Ice

reach across the table to take her hand. The touch makes her sniffle.

"Come on, Mom, tell me. What's going on?"

"Your father and I, we have... well, we have a few problems. Nothing dramatic. But it's bothering me a little."

"What kind of problems?"

"Oh, as I said, nothing dramatic. It'll be fine. Let's drop the subject." She doesn't say anything more about it, and I don't press further. I know my mother well enough to understand that she won't discuss this with me. That's how my parents have always been. No matter how bad their fights got, they never let me feel it. Admittedly, until today, I was perfectly fine with them keeping me out of their arguments. But now, seeing how desperate my mother is, I feel like I need to get involved. I'll grill Dad about it when I'm back in Portland. He's more likely to spill the beans than Mom. Whatever problem they have, it would be a surprise if there wasn't a solution.

"Okay, you don't have to talk about it. But you should know that I'm here for you if you need me," I say softly, stroking the back of her hand. "If there's anything I can do, just let me know." She nods and gets up to get a tissue.

"Thank you, my darling. Hey, weren't you supposed to meet Riley today?" she diverts from the topic.

"Yes, we were planning to go to the mall with Mason and get some stuff for the New Year's Eve party. Speaking of Riley; can I use your phone to call her?" I left mine in Portland. At first, I thought about asking Dad to mail it to me, but then I figured the distance from Caleb and the Devils might do me good. Now, I'm trying to get by without a phone and push away the recurring thoughts of the forward. And since nothing helps my heavy heart better than distraction, I've filled almost every free minute with plans with my friends.

"Of course, my dear." Mom picks up her phone from the

Breaking the Ice

sideboard and hands it to me.

"Thanks." I dial my friend's number and confirm our mall outing.

In the next few days, I shop extensively, dance, go to the movies, and have dinner with Riley and her quarterback, Cole. Even though I'm having a lot of fun, I can't get Caleb out of my head. I keep seeing him in front of me - how he pressed me against the glass door of the cigar shop with that intense gaze. I feel his proximity, penetrating every cell of my body. On New Year's Eve night, I dream about him. We're in front of the cigar shop again, but this time, I don't tell him to go back to Jessica; instead, I kiss him. I take what my heart desires and am rewarded with an indescribable sense of happiness. When I wake up the next morning and realize Caleb isn't by my side because I rejected him, I feel miserable. For the first time, I'm afraid I made a mistake. I think I should have let him in. Now, I've messed up and driven him back into that stupid witch's arms. My mood is at rock-bottom as I drive to Coach Klark's house for the New Year's Eve party. The old wooden house brings back memories. *Man, how many times have I celebrated here with the Washington White Sharks team. The guys are almost as cool as the Devils. But only almost,* I hear Toby say in my thoughts, *no one is as cool as we are.* I chuckle, I can't wait to go back tomorrow and see him and the others again.

"Emma, wow, you look fantastic," Jester greets me as soon as I step through the door. As always, he has his dark brown hair tied up in a bun, which, along with his full beard, gives him a hipster look. "Can I get you something to drink? Beer, wine, champagne? I think I have a bottle of champagne in my room, actually." He winks at me.

"No, thanks. I don't want anything." He doesn't need to know that I hardly drink alcohol anymore after that night at the Brillant. "Have you seen Riley?"

"Yeah, she was in the backyard a little while ago. I think she's preparing some of those lanterns for midnight."

"Thanks." I leave my ex and go through the back door into the garden illuminated by torches. The last time I was here, I sat with Riley down by the creek and poured my heart out to her, tears streaming down my face. Today, finding her almost in the same spot, I feel like crying all over again.

"Hey, Emma, are you here to help me?"

"Sure." I try to force a smile, which obviously fails.

"What's wrong?" Riley lets go of the lantern umbrella she's unfolding and looks at me with furrowed brows. Of course, I can't fool her. She knows me too well.

"Oh, it's nothing," I try to downplay it anyway because I don't want to ruin her evening with my mood. "How can I help?"

"You know I won't let it go, spill it. What's on your mind?" Sighing, I look up and meet my friend's gaze. She looks beautiful with her blonde curls, big blue eyes, and that gentle expression. I know she's glowing because she's so happy with Cole. A wave of nostalgia washes over me. Something in my heart tells me I could be just as happy with Caleb.

"Emma, you..." Two rowdy football players coming out of the back door interrupt us. They sit on the bottom step and light up a cigarette, watching us with glazed eyes. "Come." Riley takes me by the hand and leads me down the riverbank. We sit on a rock that sticks halfway out of the water. Here we're alone and can talk in peace. "So, what's going on with you? Is it about that hockey guy? Caleb?"

I look at her in surprise. While I've told her a lot about him, I've never let on that I have feelings for him. Otherwise, she would have grilled me the whole time. Or worse, suggested that he come over and celebrate New Year's with us. And that's exactly what I didn't want. I wanted distance to finally get him out of my head.

"How do you know it's about Caleb?"

"Emma, sweetheart, I've known you for almost my entire life. Do you really think I can't tell when something's bothering you?"

"Then why didn't you say anything?"

"Because I didn't want to pressure you. But I have a feeling you've been feeling worse these past few days."

I press my lips together and nod.

"So, what's going on with this Caleb?" I sigh, take a moment to consider where to start, and then pour my heart out to my friend.

"I told you about that playoff party, right?"

"The one at Caleb's loft, yes."

I nod.

"At that party, I met his girlfriend, Jessica. She's a beast, completely lost it because I'm the new masseuse."

"Jealous?"

"Very much so. Anyway, she started insulting and berating me."

"Even though she didn't even know you? What a bitch."

"Mhm. She called me a whore, so I threw my soda in her face."

Riley grins. I know what she's thinking: *Typical Emma. Well done!*

"But that's not the point. After that, I took off and Caleb followed me." The cigar shop comes to my mind again, and how he held me captive between his arms. God, I feel like I can smell him, that's how vivid the memory is. "He made me admit that I want him. To be honest, I've wanted him from the first day. There's something special about him that captivates me. And then he said he wanted to hear exactly that."

"But that sounds good," my friend says as I gaze at the dark river beside us.

"I told him to go back to Jessica because I didn't want to be the reason their relationship fell apart."

Riley clicks her tongue in annoyance at that.

"If he chased after you instead of calming down his angry shrew, then I assume their relationship was already on the rocks."

"Probably." I shrug. "He actually wanted to go up right away that night and end things with her."

"But?"

"But I told him to leave it because I..."

"Because you didn't want to stand between him and his girlfriend, I get it," she interrupts me. I turn my gaze back to Riley, who now looks at me not with pity, but with anger. "Emma, I know you despise women who deliberately push themselves into relationships and destroy them. But with Caleb and Jessica, there was nothing left to destroy. That was obvious. I hate to repeat myself, but the guy left his girl hanging and chased after you. Hello! You don't do that if your partner means anything to you."

I have to agree with her. And thinking back, it was really sweet of him to chase after me. He left all his guests just for me. A warm feeling spreads in my chest, and my brain starts working. Caleb really intended to leave Jessica that night. I saw it in his eyes. He was serious. Damn, he even shouted after me. The memory of the desperate sound of his voice sends shivers down my arms. *Damn, I made a mistake. A damn stupid mistake! At least it's not my decision whether he's had enough of Jessica or not and whether he wants me. I wouldn't have taken him away from her. In truth, she had already lost him.* A disgusting pull awakens in my stomach. What have I done?

"What's going through your mind?" my friend's voice reaches me.

"That I made a mistake."

"Hallelujah, you got it. And now, what's your plan?"

"No idea," I'd rather cry.

"Alright, then I'll tell you what you're going to do." Riley leans in close, looking at me firmly in the eyes. "You're going to go back to Portland tomorrow and set things right. You'll tell Caleb that you've had time to think about it, and you've changed your mind."

"And what if he's still with Jessica?"

"Whether they're together or not doesn't matter. This is solely about you telling him what you really feel. If you don't, you'll regret it forever, wondering what you let slip through your fingers." Riley's right. I need to tell him how I feel – admit that I made a mistake. I lean forward, hugging my friend. "And with a woman who called you a whore, you don't need to have any pity," she adds firmly.

"Thank you," I say against her blonde hair.

"Always," she replies gently. "And now," she says with a grin as I let her go, "let's party."

The New Year's Eve party at Coach Klark's holiday home is amazing. Alec grills burgers for everyone, trying to convince us they taste better with strawberry jam than with ketchup. Mason spends the whole evening with his phone in hand, video calling his girlfriend in Germany, and Riley and I dance until our feet are sore with Cole and a few others in the living room. At midnight, a few defensive players set off a massive firework display that must have cost several hundred dollars. It's an unforgettable evening, and even though I miss Caleb, I enjoy spending New Year's with my friends.

The goodbye the next day is hard – especially with Mom. By the time I've said goodbye to everyone and hit the road, it's early afternoon. During the drive, I contemplate what I'll say to Caleb. It's not so easy, because every time I think about

Breaking the Ice

seeing him again, countless butterflies distract me, swirling through my stomach.

In Portland, I'm greeted by Dad. He spent his first Christmas without his family and is sentimental. To celebrate, he's cooked for us. I'd love to call Caleb first, but my phone isn't on the nightstand where I remember leaving it before heading to Aberdeen. Dad calls that the food will be ready in five minutes, so I have to wait a bit longer to make the call. I quickly jump in the shower before sitting at the table in my bathrobe. We have spaghetti Bolognese, or rather overcooked pasta with a sauce that tastes slightly burnt. But hey, it's the thought that counts. For his sake, I force myself to eat everything while we chat. He wants to know how Aberdeen was, what's new with Riley, and how I spent New Year's. He doesn't say a word about Mom. Just as I'm about to broach the subject, he starts telling me about his time here. How he hardly had to massage anyone over the holidays, partly because Caleb had a motorcycle accident. My fork slips from my hand.

"What? When?" Dad looks at me, surprised by my horror.

"The night of the playoff party." Oh my God. My throat tightens, and my heart painfully clenches.

"What happened? Please tell me he's okay." My father furrows his brow, but answers, "He was at the Brillant and drank way too much. I think they even had to pump his stomach at the hospital. Anyway, he went off the road on his way back with his motorcycle."

I have to press my hands against my lips to keep from crying out in despair.

"Emma, what's wrong?"

What's wrong? I made the biggest mistake of my life. I rejected the man I desire more than anything and am responsible for his accident. *There's no doubt in my mind. I'm to blame!*

"How is he?" I ask with a choked voice.

Breaking the Ice

"He's better now. He had to stay in the hospital for a few days. As far as I know, he was lucky, just a few scrapes."

Oh, thank you, God, thank you!

"I didn't know you cared so much about this guy. Are you two together?"

"No, it's... complicated."

"Complicated..." Dad's phone rings, prompting him to get up and take it from the kitchen counter where it's charging.

"Bill! Hey, everything alright?... What?... I see... Sure, I'll come. Be there in ten minutes."

"Everything okay?" I inquire as he takes the car keys from the shelf.

"Durand pulled a thigh muscle. I have to go check it out. We'll talk later?"

"Sure."

Dad is barely out the door when I shoot up and head to my room. Like a madwoman, I search the room for my phone. I find it in the gap between my bed's headboard and the mattress. It probably slipped in there while I was packing. As feared, the battery is dead. Damn! With trembling hands, I dig my charger out of the suitcase and plug the phone in. Then I wait impatiently, tapping my toes, until it has enough juice to turn on. It takes an eternity, but finally, it boots up. The minutes feel like hours. When it finally does, I see 497 WhatsApp messages, 49 missed calls, and 2 text messages. On an inner impulse, I open the texts first. Both are from Caleb!

First message received on December 22 at 9:36 PM:

I've left Jessica.

My stomach glows with excitement. He left her. He actually left her!

Second message received on December 22 at 9:37 PM:

*Emma, the only woman in this world that I want is you. I

144

won't accept your 'no' any longer. You belong to me, and you know it.

"Caleb," I whisper as I sit on the bed, reading the messages again. I can hardly believe my luck. He's free, he actually left Jessica. Now nothing stands in our way. I press the phone to my chest, realizing something: Caleb sent me these messages eleven days ago. He'll think I intentionally didn't reply because I still don't want him. Damn it, I should have had the phone shipped to me. What if he got fed up with the whole thing? The thought terrifies me. Please, I can't mess this up again just because I forgot my phone! I feverishly think about what to do. The easiest would be to call him directly to sort things out. But it feels wrong. Before I realize what I'm doing, I throw on some clothes, unplug my phone, and head to Caleb's loft.

16

CALEB

At eight in the evening, a knock echoes at my apartment door. I assume it's the pizza delivery, so I open it, hardly believing who I find standing there.

"Emma," I exclaim in surprise, stepping into the corridor and pulling the door slightly shut behind me.

"Caleb, I..." she starts, but doesn't continue. Instead, she looks at me, breathing heavily. She seems agitated, her eyes are reddened, as if she's been crying. And then, entirely unexpectedly, she closes the gap between us, wrapping her hands around my neck and kisses me. For a moment, I'm taken aback. But then, I feel her velvety lips against mine. I lift my hands, cradling the back of her head, pouring all the pain and longing of the past weeks into this kiss. Underneath me, Emma makes a relieved sound. Her fingers grip my hair, while her tongue presses insistently against my lips. I part them, inviting her in, rewarded with the incredible taste of her. It makes me lose control, pressing her against the wall. She gasps into my mouth as I press my hips against hers, making her feel what she's doing to me. I never thought I'd be this close to her again. And yet, here she is, clouding my senses with her taste and proximity.

Breaking the Ice

This woman makes me block out everything else around us, heightening my desire to an almost painful level. So, I kiss her more urgently, let my hands roam up her exquisite butt, and pull her closer. Through the thin sweater she wears under her open jacket, I can feel that her nipples are hard. Fuck. In my mind, a thought arises, pushing everything else aside.

I want this woman in my bed!

I release her mouth, kissing and licking my way over her chin and down her neck to her collarbone. My fingers glide up from her amazing ass, just about to settle on her breasts when her hands intercept mine.

"Wait, Caleb," Emma gasps. I straighten up, looking at her with desire-clouded eyes. "I'm actually here to talk."

"Talk?" After that kiss, there's nothing more to talk about. The matter is crystal clear, this woman belongs to me. And I won't let her go for anything in the world.

"Let's go inside."

"This is rather inconvenient at the moment," I say, making a remorseful face. My words throw a horrified expression onto Emma's face. I can see her peering towards the apartment door, suddenly going pale.

"Oh God, no, damn it, this can't be true," she says, trying to push me away. I hold her fast, utterly bewildered, and then it dawns on me what her problem is.

"You think I have another woman here." Emma blinks at me, her eyes teary.

"Not at all?"

"Absolutely not! Tonight is poker night with the guys. I thought I'd spare you their curious gazes and send them away first."

"The guys..." she repeats, seeming to finally understand.

"If you don't mind them bombarding you with silly remarks, feel free to come in," I say, motioning towards the door.

Breaking the Ice

She presses her lips together, looking undecided.

"Caleb, are you telling the pizza guy your life story? Why is this taking so long? I'm starving!" Toby's voice reaches us.

"Toby's here too?" she asks.

"Yeah, the little cheat swindles us every week." She takes a moment to think and then says, "Alright, you know what, forget it. I'll come along. I'm used to the guys and their dumb comments."

"Perfect, then come on in." I take her small hand in my huge one and lead her into my apartment. Parker, Toby, Byers, and the new defender Peters are sitting at the poker table across from the kitchen. Each of them has their jaw dropping when they see who I've brought along.

"Emma, sweetheart, you're back!" Toby greets her happily, stands up, and comes over to us to envelop her in his massive arms. "Mandy and I were worried. We tried to reach you at least a dozen times," he scolds.

"Sorry, I left my phone in Portland," she says with an apologetic look. Ah, that explains why she hasn't responded to my messages until now.

"Alright, guys, the party's over," I announce, indicating for them to leave. I can't wait to be alone with Emma. The sooner they're out, the better!

"What? But we just got here," complains Byers.

"Exactly! And besides, I've got an unbeatable hand." Peters waves his cards. *Like I care.*

"Alright, you don't have to leave on my account," Emma interjects. What? "I'm happy to watch." *No, hell no, this way they will never leave.*

"Or you could join in," Parker suggests, smiling at her conciliatorily. What a jerk! I shoot him a deadly look, which he ignores, and he offers Emma the empty chair beside him. I have no choice but to watch as she and Toby sit down and start chatting.

The next two hours feel like the longest of my life. Emma sits across from me, sending me deep looks from her cat-like eyes, making sure I'm constantly aroused. And when she stretches her foot under the table towards me, running it up my leg, I'm on the brink of losing it. I have to restrain myself from flipping the poker table like a caveman, throwing her over my shoulder, and carrying her upstairs to my bed. It's hard for me to follow the game. I lose round after round because I only have eyes for her. Just after ten, my patience is wearing thin. I want some privacy now! So, I wait until we finish the round and then collect the cards.

"Alright, guys, that's it. We're done for today," I declare.

"Oh, come on, it was just getting good. Just one more round," Byers pleads, clinking his chips.

"You've swiped three quarters of my stake, so quit your whining," I retort.

"Yeah, but only three quarters. There's more to be had," he argues.

"Cut it out, you vulture. You can bleed us dry again next week," Parker chimes in, patting Byers on the shoulder.

"Fine by me. But then we're doubling the stakes!" This gets everyone at the table, except for me, laughing. They rise at a snail's pace, slipping into their jackets. I'd love to give each of them a swift kick in the ass. They know perfectly well that I want to be alone with Emma! When I finally slam the apartment door shut behind them, I lock it and grab Emma, who's standing beside me. I pull her close and kiss her. Fuck, it feels so good to have her in my arms.

"We were supposed to talk," she mumbles against my mouth, a mischievous smile playing on her lips.

"Later," I growl, urging her towards the kitchen. I actually want to take her upstairs to my bedroom, but her tongue, plunging into my mouth, makes me abandon that plan. Instead, I head for the poker table. Reluctantly, I tear myself away from her to sweep cards and chips off the table. Then, with swift hands, I strip off her sweater and jeans. It's insane, when she stands before me in her black lingerie, I can hardly believe my luck. I grab her, lifting her up and placing her on the table. Emma raises her hands, wrapping them around my neck and pulling me down to her. Our lips find each other, and our tongues begin a wet, fiery dance. Her taste is fantastic, driving me crazy. I doubt I'll ever get enough of it. Without releasing her delicious mouth, I reach for the clasp of her bra. She shudders as I slide the straps down her arms and then remove the entire piece. Then, I kiss and lick my way down her neck, enfolding her breasts in my hands, her pierced nipples. They're perfect, fitting just right in my palms. This woman is tailor-made for me. Emma reaches for my shirt, beginning to undo it. However, she only manages three buttons before I close my mouth around one of her dark, erect buds and bite down. A cry of pleasure escapes her, which I turn into a whimper by sucking sharply on her nipple. The metal of her piercing feels exciting in my mouth. I've been with many tattooed women, but none with piercings. Emma's hands travel up to my head, where her fingers dig into my curls and grip tightly. The slight pain further arouses me, so I can't take it any longer. I want to feel her, bury my cock inside her, finally have what I've desired for so long. But first, I have to taste her. Since our first kiss in front of her house, I've been obsessed with the thought of sampling her other lips. I'm convinced that she tastes even more irresistible between her thighs. So, I pull away and kiss her once more, exploring her mouth with my tongue to etch her flavor into my memory. Meanwhile, I hook my fingers into the waistband of her panties. Emma understands and lifts her hips, allowing me to slide off her underwear.

Breaking the Ice

"If your pussy tastes as I imagine, you'll have to force me to stop," I murmur, looking down at her. In response, she bites her lip and gazes up at me seductively through her dark lashes. I dive down, kissing a path over her hard nipples, down her stomach and navel, until I reach her mound. While Emma supports herself with her hands on the table behind her, she watches me as I drape her tattooed legs over my shoulders. This gives me better access to her... wow... pierced pussy. I'm quite astonished when I discover not one, but three pieces of jewelry. A stud through the skin above her clit, and two rings, one through each inner labia. Fuck, how hot is this woman? I bet she's unbeatable in bed. I intend to find out and lightly bite into her right inner thigh. It gives her goosebumps. Then, I tease her with numerous wet kisses, drawing nearer to her most intimate spot. When I drag my tongue through the crevice where her thigh ends, she tenses up with anticipation.

"Caleb, please," she breathes. Damn, countless times I've envisioned what it would be like to hear those two words from her mouth. Now that she's said them, I want to hear them again. I want her to moan my name, to beg for me, to fuck her. That's why I lower my tongue onto her clit, gently tracing a circle around her pearl. Once again I feel her tense beneath me. I realize she can barely bear these light touches. So, I apply more pressure, causing her to soften. I lift my hands and wrap them around her thighs, securing a firm grip. Then, I take what I desire most. Her essence. My tongue delves into her cleft, savoring her. Damn, I knew it. She tastes incredible! Even as her flavor spreads across my tongue, the synapses in my brain fire. I realize that this woman has a damn high addictive potential. I eagerly run my tongue along the entire length of her vulva. Emma's gaze, clouded with desire, is fixed on me, urging me to give her more. I let my tongue flutter over her pearl before closing my lips around it and sucking gently.

Breaking the Ice

Emma gasps and tilts her head back. I feel her labia swelling beneath me, noticing she's becoming even wetter. That's how I like it. I release my right hand from her thigh and slide my index and middle fingers over her dripping entrance. As I push my fingers into her, a raw sound of pleasure escapes, Emma. She lifts her head, watching me with flushed cheeks as I lick her and stimulate her. She arches her back, pressing her pelvis against my face. It turns me on immensely. The combination of tasting her and witnessing her unrestrained desire is almost too much for me. "Caleb... yes," she gasps, reaching for my hair and clutching it tightly. I feel her muscles tighten around my fingers, and I observe her nipples constricting even more firmly. She's on the brink of orgasm. "Oh, damn it, Caleb, YES!" she moans. As I push her over the edge, and she comes on my face. Her salty essence runs warm over my lips and chin. Fuck, I can't help but lift her ass off the edge of the table and towards me. Kneeling on the floor, I savor her femininity. I absorb what she offers me, while she sits heavily on my face, breathing deeply.

17

EMMA

Out of breath, I look down at myself. With Caleb's curls in my hands, I am sitting on his face. Oh my God, never before has a man licked me like this. What he did with his tongue, with his mouth, was... sensational! Just as I try to slide off him, he lifts me off himself. I stand there with trembling legs, watching him, a grin spreading across his lips. Then he rises, never taking his eyes off me, and kisses me. He smells of sex, of me. "And now, round two," he says with a husky voice, grabbing me and throwing me over his shoulder.

"Caleb!" I exclaim in surprise, to which he responds with a smack on my bare ass. "I'm not done with you yet," he declares, leading me to the stairs and carrying me up to his bedroom. There, he places me on the bed and takes a step back. As he unbuttons his shirt and slowly sheds each piece of clothing, he devours me with his gaze. And I do too, take in his body. His broad chest, the defined abdomen, and the powerful legs. To further stoke the flames, I let my hands wander down over my breasts and between my legs. "Fuck, Emma," he growls, pulling off his black boxer shorts. My smile turns into a lascivious grin. Insane - that's what I call loaded! He gets into bed and approaches me. His hands replace mine, brushing gently like a wingbeat from my stomach upward between my breasts. Then he tugs at one of my nipple piercings - sending a hot surge between my thighs - and comes over me. Leaning on his left forearm, he uses his knee to push my legs apart, while I take the opportunity to touch him. From the massages, I'm familiar with his body. I know his muscles are firm. Yet, he feels different now, somehow more intense. My fingers glide over the smooth skin of his chest, while his heat scorches my body. "I quite like these," he whispers, running his free hand over my pubic area, where he plays with the piercings. "And this one here..." He inserts two fingers into me, triggering a wave of desire. "...I'm dangerously close to becoming addicted to." With that, he withdraws his fingers, puts them in his mouth, and sucks my wetness from them. I impatiently bite the inside of my cheek, unable to wait any longer, eager for more of him. So, I reach for his cock and spread the pre-cum I find there over his tip. This makes him sharply inhale. Before I can let my hand wander down his shaft, he reaches down and holds me back.

"If you don't want me to lose control and fuck you harder than we both might like, you'll stop that," he warns, visibly trying to restrain himself. It's hard for me to suppress a grin. Caleb raises his arm over my head and retrieves a condom packet from his nightstand. "Oh, the gentleman is prepared," I remark. But Caleb says nothing in return, only lustfully gazes at me as he impatiently takes the condom from the packet and rolls it on. Barely having it on, he positions his tip at my entrance. His impatience is almost palpable. But I too can't wait to finally feel him. So, I wrap my legs around his lower back and tease him to finally take me. "I've waited for this too long," he murmurs. A hoarse moan escapes my lips as he swiftly slides into me. My muscles wrap around him, eagerly welcoming him. "Fuck, you're so tight," he gasps, before starting to thrust into me at a brisk pace. I let go, surrendering to the moment. My body and desire take over, urging my hips towards him hungrily. I pull his handsome face down to mine, kissing him, while my fingernails trace paths across his back. We spur each other on, rolling over the bed in our passion. At times, I'm on top, riding him, and then I'm beneath him, as he thrusts deeply into me. At some point, I turn him one time too many and we tumble along with the sheets out of the bed. I want to get up, climb back on, but Caleb won't let me. Instead, he presses me onto the cool hardwood floor. His strong hands grip my hips as he thrusts into me relentlessly. His expression is marked by lust. I can feel he's on the edge. That's why I slide my right hand between my legs and rub over my swollen clit. I feel the metal of the piercing, adding an extra level of stimulation. Closing my eyes, I savor the signs of the orgasm slowly building within me. Caleb groans roughly above me, sending a cool rush of air over my stiffened nipples. That does it for me. The world around me shatters as I cry out Caleb's name once more during an earth-shattering climax. It seems to push him over the edge too. I feel him bury himself in me one final time, with a guttural sound. His cock twitches and pulses as he comes. I observe him, watching the tense expression melt away from his sharply defined features. His face softens, and a contented gleam lights up his brown eyes. *He looks incredibly handsome.*

"What's going on? Why are you smiling so mischievously?" he asks, gently brushing a strand of hair from my forehead. Oh, I hadn't even realized I was smiling at him.

"Well," I say, "I was just thinking that we should have done this sooner." To emphasize my words, I engage my lower abdominal muscles around his intimate area.

"Indeed," he agrees, lowering his lips to mine with a grin.

His kiss is tender, sending a delightful shiver down my arms and legs. Our moment is interrupted by the sound of my phone ringing downstairs.

"That must be my dad," I explain, gently pushing Caleb away. While he removes the condom and slips into his boxers, I head downstairs where my phone has just fallen silent. The fog in my mind is slowly clearing.

"What's wrong? Are you already leaving?" he asks, surprised, as he follows me and sees me getting dressed. "I thought you were going to stay the night."

"Another time, gladly. But I have to get up early tomorrow, I have a massage appointment at nine," I reply. Even though I'd like to stay, I need some time to process what I just did. It's not that it felt wrong, no, it was amazing. But for the first time in my life, and consciously at that, I broke one of my most important rules. I slept with a man just because he turned my head. Normally, I take ample time to get to know the guys I let into my pants. Often, it becomes clear after just a few days what idiots they are. Like Jester. But with Caleb, it was different. I came here already with the thought of sleeping with him.

"Will I see you tomorrow?" he inquires as he accompanies me to the door. My phone, which is ringing again, beats me to the answer. I pull it out of my pocket and glance at the display. It's Mom. Damn, I forgot to call her and let her know I arrived safely in Portland. I dismiss the call and look up at Caleb.

"I'm sorry, I have to go," I say apologetically, standing on my tiptoes to give him a farewell kiss on the lips. Before I can pull away and leave, his hands cradle my face and hold me back. Shoulders raised; he kisses me again. But unlike mine, his kiss is intense, with tongue, almost taking my breath away. When he finally releases me, my knees are weak. "Well, then, see you tomorrow," I say a little dazed and step into the hallway. Then I make sure to get away before I change my mind

Breaking the Ice

and stay.

Back home, I send Mom and Riley a message – letting them know I'm doing well. Then I plop down in front of the TV with Dad. When he asks where I've been, I say I was with Mandy. He doesn't need to know about Caleb just yet. Not until I know if there's anything serious between the center and me. Lost in thought, I stare at the TV with vacant eyes for a while before retreating to my room. I lie awake almost the entire night, sorting through my thoughts like large stacks of paper, shuffling them back and forth, weighing what's right and what's wrong. *Was it a mistake to get involved with Caleb so quickly and sleep with him? Who knows if he's serious about us, if I can trust him.* Just before dawn, my eyes finally close.

When my phone alarm wakes me up at seven-thirty, I surprisingly feel refreshed. And more than that, I can't wait to go to work and see Caleb again. While I hop in the shower, I go through the thought stacks from last night once more. I've decided for myself that it was okay to sleep with him so soon. What I feel for Caleb, I've never felt for any other man before. What's between us is unique. And for that very reason, I've decided to open myself up to him without reservations. I know it makes me vulnerable. After all, I don't know him that well. It's entirely possible that this is all just a game for him. But I'm willing to take that risk. Besides, there's this quiet feeling in my heart that tells me Caleb feels the same way.

After a breakfast where I let Dad fill me in on what he's been up to over the holidays – he was either at home or with Bill – we head to the ice rink. My first appointment today is at nine with Byers. Since I'm fifteen minutes early, I don't go straight down to my massage room. Instead, I glance at the ice rink. Who knows, maybe I'll be lucky and run into Caleb. As far as I know, he often trains around this time. Unfortunately, the ice rink is deserted, so I head downstairs disappointed. On the stairs, I'm considering whether to send Caleb a message when I hear his voice.

"No, Jessica, that changes nothing," I hear him say in exasperation. *Jessica, his ex?* I press myself against the staircase wall and peer around the corner in the direction of his voice. Sure enough, I spot Caleb and his ex-girlfriend a few meters further down the hall. He has his arms crossed over his chest and looks standoffish, while she holds her folded hands against her heart. She looks up at him with a pleading expression.

"Just tell me what I can do to get you back to me. Please, Caleb, I need you," she pleads, reaching out a hand to him, but he backs away.

"Please understand. There's nothing you can do."

"But, Caleb, if you just give me a chance, it could be like it was before and..."

"Damn it, Jess!" he cuts her off harshly. "How many times do I have to tell you? It's over between us. I don't want this anymore! Get that through your head." With that, he pushes past her, trying to leave her behind, but Jessica clings desperately to his arm.

"You can't do that, Caleb. That's not fair, please, I..." Shit, Jessica spotted me – and now Caleb too.

"Um, hi," I greet them awkwardly, approaching the two. "I'm sorry, I didn't mean to interrupt."

"But you did," the blonde hisses, glaring at me through teary eyes.

"She didn't," Caleb interjects, disentangling himself from his ex-girlfriend, coming towards me and pulling me into his arms. As he greets me with a kiss, I hear Jessica audibly inhale in anger behind him.

"Well, well," she sneers maliciously. "So, Durand was right after all. You did manage to seduce the bitch." Her insult prompts Caleb to release me and turn to face her.

"You should be careful with your words," he warns her in a tone that even makes me feel queasy. Then, he wraps his arm around my back like a protective shield and pulls me possessively close.

"Oh, is that so? Well, I'm more of the opinion that this little doll here should be the one on the lookout. Specifically, who she gets involved with."

"Is that a threat?" I ask, raising an eyebrow. This woman must be out of her mind!

"No, it's an advice. Even if you probably don't deserve it." She wrinkles her nose and looks down at me in disgust. "You should know, masseuse, that Caleb only stays with women as long as they're useful to him."

I feel him tense at her words.

"You better leave now," he growls.

"No, I'll go when I'm finished here. This man here..." Jessica, accusatorily points her finger at Caleb. "...Only uses women for his own purposes. Thanks to me, he managed to get onto the team. As soon as he had a secure position, he dropped me like shit. He doesn't care about anyone else's feelings. For him, only one thing matters: his success." What?

"That's not true," he grumbles over me, but Jessica ignores him and continues, "Maybe you should consider what advantage he's hoping to gain from you."

She adopts a pitying expression and shakes her head regretfully. "Whatever it is, I can promise you one thing: once he's achieved his goal, even if it's just to get in your pants, he'll disappear. Believe me, you're not doing yourself any favors with this man. With him by your side, you can only lose."

Her gaze returns to Caleb. She loses some of her maliciousness and takes on a somewhat sorrowful expression. Then, she passes us without a word of goodbye and disappears. I'm so taken aback that I can only blink up at Caleb. His gaze is fixed

Breaking the Ice

on the stairs, down which Jessica has just vanished. A muscle twitches in his jaw and there's a look of intense hatred burning in his eyes.

"What did she mean by that?" I need to know if this was just the accusations of a jealous bitch or if I've really gotten involved with a selfish jerk. With his lips pressed into a line, Caleb shakes his head. *What is it? Is it a no-that's-not-true shake or a what-have-I-done shake?* Confused, I extricate myself from him and head down the hallway towards the massage room.

"Emma, wait," I hear him behind me.

"I have a massage, Caleb. We'll talk later, when you've figured out what you want to say." With quick strides, I turn the corner and see Byers waiting outside my room. "I'm sorry, I'm late," I apologize to him.

He waves it off. "No worries, I just got here."

As I retrieve the key from my bag to unlock the door, Caleb catches up to me.

"Emma, let's talk about this," he urges.

"As I said, I have work to do." I smile at the defender and hold the door open for him.

Before he can enter, Caleb grabs him by the upper arm and holds him back. "Hey man, do you think we could switch appointments for once? You can take mine at ten." Byers furrows his brow, looking puzzled between the two of us.

"Sure," he eventually says, shrugging. "I'll just train first and get the massage afterwards."

"Thanks, I owe you one."

Byers heads off, and Caleb ushers me into the room. As he switches on the light and closes the door behind him, I put some distance between us by stepping behind the massage table.

"So?" I ask, crossing my arms. "What's the deal with Jessica's accusations?"

Breaking the Ice

Caleb sighs. "How much time do we have?"

"An hour."

"Okay, that'll have to do." And then Caleb tells me his story. I learn that he's been playing hockey since childhood, that the sport was the most important thing in his life for a long time. He explains that in Two Rivers, the town he's from, there was no opportunity for him to showcase his talent. I find out how he met Jessica. Initially, he was actually only interested in getting close to her father. So, in that regard, she didn't lie. He also tells me how Jessica fell in love with him, and how he couldn't bring himself to leave her when he achieved his goal and made it onto the team. Caleb is brutally honest. He talks and talks, and the longer I listen, the clearer two things become to me. Firstly, even though he tries to sugarcoat it, he did use this girl for his own benefit. And secondly, he really wants me to believe that he's not a bad person. Obviously, he feels more for me than I realized. But is that enough for me? No. Even if I'm infatuated with him, I can't change who I am. I want nothing to do with people who exploit others for their own gain. Even though Caleb insists time and time again that he's changed, I don't believe him. *Once an asshole, always an asshole,* I think.

"Emma, please say something," he pleads softly, after finishing and I'm silently staring at him. There's a vulnerable look in his brown eyes that cuts right to my heart. Even though I know I should, I can't bring myself to completely end things between us. So, I say, "You should go now. I need time to think." Caleb is in the midst of running his hand through his hair in a desperate gesture when there's a knock at the door. Byers sticks his head in.

"The hour is up, it's my turn," he says, coming inside. "And no, Whyler, don't even think about sending me away again. I need my massage, right now. Got a date later." While the defender takes a seat on the massage table and circles his tense shoulders, Caleb continues to look at me expectantly. I know he can't accept my decision, but that's what he'll have to do. He exhales sharply through his nose and glances resignedly to the side when he realizes I won't give in.

"Please, for my sake," he says icily, turns on his heel, and leaves. He doesn't even look back as Byers calls after him, "Hey, Whyler, don't forget Toby's birthday party tomorrow night! Eight o'clock at the Brillant!" My heart feels like a lump of lava. Oh God, I want to cry.

18

CALEB

If there ever was a day that could be chalked up as a complete washout, it's today. After my futile attempts to persuade Emma that I'm not the douchebag she believes me to be, everything took a turn for the worse. Firstly, I collided with Parker during the morning training session, as he prodded for details about my previous evening. Then, Coach Thornton left no room for praise during the video analysis. And truth be told, he was on the mark; I just couldn't seem to find my stride today. To cap it off, I narrowly avoided turning my freshly mended bike into scrap metal during a hairpin turn. All day, I've been in a state of disarray, my mind unfocused. Now, I'm pacing back and forth in my living room. It's inconceivable that Jessica might be the harbinger of doom for my chances with Emma. I contemplate whether reaching out to Jess could be of any use. *And then what?* Sneers the unkind voice in my head. *What are you going to say to her? 'Please, assist me in winning back Emma?' Insist that it wasn't meant in that manner?* Fuck! There's simply no turn of phrase that would coax her into helping me. On the contrary, she'd likely find a way to drive a deeper wedge between us. No, I certainly won't be seeking Jessica's counsel. *Perhaps*, I should try giving Emma a call, attempting to engage her in conversation. No, that's a notion just as ill-conceived. She requested time to think. If I press her now, I risk sending her packing for good.

"Fuck!" I roar, hurling my phone onto the couch. It bounces off the cushion and clatters to the floor. I rub my temples, contemplating what could serve as a distraction. I don't want to face the guys right now. Given my mood, one wrong word and I might just lose it. Riding my motorcycle again doesn't appeal either. I've been out on it for three hours already today.

So, I decide to hit the hay before I'm tempted to reach for the bottle and repeat the same mistake as the night of the playoff party. It turns out to be a grueling night. I wake up repeatedly, glancing at my phone each time. I'm hoping for a message from Emma. All in vain. The next morning, I feel utterly drained, and my foul mood is even irritating me. To spare my buddies, I decide to hit the weight room and channel my aggression. I actually train until I'm so depleted that the barbell slips from my hand. Holding onto a glimmer of hope that I might run into Emma, I spend the entire day at the ice rink. To my disappointment, I only run into her father. My last hope is Toby's birthday party tonight. And indeed, she's there. My chest tightens painfully as I spot her in a jaw-dropping black dress in the VIP area. She's seated between the birthday boy and Parker. He's grinning at her like an idiot while they chat. I can feel the jealousy surging within me. Though he's my friend, I don't entirely trust him. To be honest, I don't trust anyone when it comes to Emma. So, I make haste, passing by the security guards and heading up to the VIP area. I greet the others and congratulate Toby. He's delighted with the bottle of Irish whiskey I brought him and invites me for a beer. We've barely placed our order when Byers and a few of the defensemen arrive. I leave them with Toby and settle into the armchair diagonally across from Emma. She's already noticed me and offers a smile my way. I wonder if she's had enough time to mull everything over. Damn, I hope so! Unfortunately, she doesn't seem inclined to come over and talk. That's tough. The waiter brings my beer, which I take a big swig of while studying her. She's wearing golden earrings that resemble tiny leaves. They cascade almost to her shoulders, glimmering with her movements. Her dress hugs her body like a second skin. It's shorter than the last one but has long sleeves to compensate. When she briefly turns to Toby, I catch a glimpse of the deep back neckline. I take another gulp, washing away the dryness in my throat. Perhaps I should leave, spare myself the pain of being so close yet so far. But I can't bring myself to do it. Instead, I sit there like a damned masochist, gazing at her. Her face is dangerously beautiful! Those dark, smoldering eyes...

"Durand!" Toby's voice snaps me out of it. I glance over at him. The Canadian is shaking our goalie's hand, and he's got none other than Jessica in tow. *Well, look at that, she's found a new direction rather quickly, considering how desperately she wanted me back,* I think to myself, shaking my head in disbelief. I watch the two of them as they sit down, and she snuggles up to him. *Well, they're actually a perfect match,* I contemplate. *Like toilet paper and... well, you get the idea.* I redirect my attention to Emma, who is also observing the newcomers. I wonder what's going through her mind now.

"Listen up, everyone!" Toby calls out, handing his sweetheart a monstrous piece of that triangular Swiss chocolate we all love. Mandy needs both hands for that monstrosity. "As the Devils' betting officer, I have an announcement to make! Parker and Durand approached me with a request to settle their bet before the agreed-upon date!"

And I know exactly why they want that. They're scared stiff. I know from Parker that the thought of facing his personal lit-

Breaking the Ice

tle puck hell at the end of the season is eating away at him. The two of them want to get it over with. "And so, after careful consideration..." Toby pauses dramatically, then raises his hands authoritatively. "... I've decided to grant their request and move the date to tomorrow night at eight o'clock!" Applause erupts, which Toby, in his role as betting officer, solemnly acknowledges. Internally, I chuckle. *Show-off. All that's left is for him to take a bow.* He sits back down with his girlfriend, who plants a kiss on him, then gets up and goes over to Emma. At first, I think she intends to squeeze herself in between my girl and Parker. But then I see her extend her hand, pulling Emma to her feet. Emma shoots me a brief, electrifying glance as she passes by with Mandy. Fuck! It's only now that I notice how deep the back of her dress is cut. The fabric barely covers her butt. My cock responds automatically as my gaze travels up her spine, discovering a tattoo I'm unfamiliar with. It's a kind of tribal design from which a rose blossoms. Is that new, or was it already there two days ago when she writhed beneath me in my bed? I can't recall seeing it. A thought stirs in my mind. A promise to myself. *If I manage to get this woman in my bed again, I'll explore every inch of her body. That's as certain as the Amen in church.*

I watch Mandy and Emma, who are heading downstairs past the security guards, making their way to the dance floor. Dammit, in this dress, she'll practically be inviting men to touch her on the dance floor. My hands start to sweat with anger. I should follow her, make sure no one gets too close.

"Well, Whyler!" Durand's voice interrupts my thoughts. He stands above me, wearing a smug grin and holding a bottle of beer. What does he want now? I get up, not liking the way he's looking down on me.

"What do you want, Durand?" Standing tall, it's me now looking down at him. But that doesn't seem to faze him; he

Breaking the Ice

still regards me with that smug expression.

"Looks like I'll soon be Mr. Flake's favorite," he remarks.

"Because you're banging his daughter?" I retort with a laugh. "Keep dreaming." While Carl wasn't exactly thrilled that I left Jess, it hasn't changed my position as his star forward. He knows I'm his best man.

"Well, you see, it's the whole package. You're sabotaging yourself. First, you lose it at Jessica's gallery opening, then you break up with her, and lately, you're even faltering in training. Looks pretty bad for you, don't you think?"

"The only thing that looks bad is the stench coming out of your mouth. Now, get out of my way." I shove the Canadian aside and stride towards the bathrooms, determined to avoid any confrontation, whether with Durand or any guy getting too close to Emma. As I approach the hallway leading to the restrooms, I'm about to pass the ladies' room when someone grabs me and pulls me inside.

"What the... Jess!" I exclaim, irritated when I see who it is. "Are you out of your mind?"

"You're about to find out," she hisses. A girl at the sink, washing her hands, spots us.

"Hey, what's this? This is the women's restroom!" she scolds.

"Yes, and this is important," Jess replies, grabbing her by the arm and roughly pushing her out the door.

"You're crazy, you stupid bitch!" the stranger grumbles, but Jess doesn't engage with her. Instead, she shuts the door behind her and leans against it, preventing anyone else from entering.

"So, what do you want?" I ask, exasperated, crossing my arms. I shouldn't even be speaking to this witch after she stirred up trouble between Emma and me yesterday.

"I want you to make a decision."

"Okay, this is ridiculous. I have no idea what's going through your crazy head, but you're definitely not going to dictate decisions to me. I'm sorry you're hurt. I'm also sorry I used you. It wasn't right of me and there's no excuse. I get that. But you have to move on from our breakup."

"Oh, I will move on, in my own way. And that's why you'll decide."

"Her or you?" I furrow my brow. *Her or me?*

"Either I ensure Emma loses her job and goes back to the backwater town she came from, or I make sure you get kicked off the team. And more than that – no hockey team in the world will ever sign you again."

"Okay, you know what, you need help. You should schedule an appointment with a psychologist." With that, I try to push her away from the door and leave, but she pushes back and screams, "You don't believe me, do you?" Then, she raises her fist and punches herself in the face so hard that the skin at the corner of her mouth tears and she starts bleeding.

"Have you completely lost your mind?!" I think I'm going insane. This woman is a freak!

"It's possible," she shrugs. "I'll disfigure myself so badly that not even my parents will recognize me. And then I'll say it was you. The police, the press, everyone will know what a psychopath you are. How do you think that will affect your career? Dad will kick you out and no one – especially not with the reputation of a woman beater – will want you."

"You wouldn't do that," I say, looking back and forth between her ice-cold eyes and her split lip.

"Think so, huh? Caleb, I've reached a point where I'd do anything. And you know what, you brought this on yourself. You should have never left me. But you thought you could replace me with that slit-eyed whore. Well, this is what you get. If I can't have you, then no one should." Jessica steps away from the door. "You have three days to decide." She turns around, grabs the handle, and is about to leave when she pauses – but she doesn't turn to me. "And, Caleb, if I don't have an answer from you by then, I'll make sure both of you get kicked out. So, you better make up your mind soon." With those words, she disappears, leaving me alone.

"Fuck!" My fist slams into the tiled wall. *This can't be happening; this lunatic is blackmailing me!* I need to get out of here, I need time to think. I have no idea how to fix this shit.

"Caleb?" I hear a soft voice behind me. Shit, I thought we were alone. I turn around and see Emma emerging from one of the stalls. There's an apologetic look on her beautiful face. She extends a hand towards me, which I grasp in surprise.

"You heard what just happened?"

"Yes, and I'm terribly sorry. I was disappointed because you took advantage of that poor girl. But Jessica doesn't deserve my sympathy at all. That woman is a complete nut job. What she just threatened you with is insane!" At this moment, my ex doesn't matter to me. I can't believe my luck. Emma has come back to me, I have her again! I pull her into my arms, burying my nose in her silky hair and closing my eyes. Never again, I promise myself, will I risk losing her.

When she eventually pulls away from me and looks up at me, my heart aches with relief.

"What will you do about Jessica?" she asks, concerned. Out of anger towards that witch, I bite down on my teeth. "I don't know yet, but I'll come up with something. I promise. Don't worry." Trying to appear composed, I gently stroke her cheek with the back of my hand. "What do you say we get out of here?"

She smiles gently. "Sounds like a plan."

I pull her back into my arms, bringing her face between my hands and kiss her. Damn, how I've missed her and her taste!

Since I want to get out of here as quickly as possible, we say our goodbyes to the birthday boy and his girlfriend and leave. The taxi ride to my loft brings back memories. It feels like an eternity since I escorted Emma home from the Brillant that first night. Back then, she seemed unreachable; today she sits snuggled up next to me. A lot has happened since then. Briefly, Jessica's threats come to mind. I urgently need to figure out a way to deal with that witch. But not today – right now, there's only one thing on my mind: having Emma in my bed.

When we arrive at the loft, I help my beauty out of her coat. Then, I pull her in for a kiss.

"Is there anything else I should know about you?" she asks when I finally let go. The question sounds playful, but I know there's a kernel of truth in it. Emma wants to make sure I don't have any more skeletons in my closet before she commits to me.

"Well, to be honest, I do have a fetish," I admit, causing her to narrow her eyes. "It's related to sex." Now, a crease forms on her forehead, but it quickly smooths out.

"Could it be related to bodily fluids?" she speculates.

"You could say that, yes. You've noticed, I take it."

"I could say that" she playfully repeats my words.

"I can't help it. You just taste too damn good," I confess, letting her feel that the thought of her juices alone gets me hard.

"Good to know." Emma grins, biting down on her lower lip. "And what else are you into?"

"The thought of coming on your pierced breasts or the tattoo above your ass almost makes me explode," I admit, hoping she won't find me repulsive because of it. Shaking my head, I lick my lips. "Now you probably think I'm a pervert." Damn, I shouldn't have said anything. Emma reaches up, takes hold of my chin, and forces me to look at her.

"I don't know how uptight the women that you had before me were – and I don't want to know! But I'm into kinky sex. Into really hot, kinky sex." The wicked grin she gives me makes me realize she has no problem with my fetish. Fuck, and I thought she couldn't get any hotter. After our last session – where she sat on my face with her pussy – I should have known she's different from other women. Emma is more uninhibited, more open. I could have seen that from her many intimate piercings.

"And now come, I want to find out how good you taste," she says in a seductive voice, taking my hand and trying to pull me towards the couch.

"Wait," I stop her with a painfully hard cock in my pants. "I promise you; I'll fuck you on every single piece of furniture in this loft, but today I want you in my bed." With that, I pull her back, lift her into my arms, and carry her upstairs.

19

EMMA

My phone's alarm rouses me from slumber. Groggily, I lift my eyelids and find Caleb lying beside me. He props his head on a bent arm, watching me.

"Good morning," I say with a smile, attempting to maneuver over him to reach my phone and turn off the alarm. Yet Caleb seizes me the moment I'm upon him, quickly maneuvering onto his back and seating me astride.

I can feel his boner between my legs.

"Yes," he answers with a grin on his lips. "Indeed, it is a good morning."

He grabs my bare breasts with both hands, leans forward and bites my left nipple. A sweet pain runs from my nipple, which erects immediately, down to my thighs. Even though we had sex all night long, I would do nothing else but start the next round.

But I can't do that because of work.

"You just can't get enough," I murmur and tease him by rubbing my already wet pussy on his erect cock. "What do you expect, with a woman like you?" he growls, grabs my butt and greedily places my pussy over the tip of his cock. Shit, now I have to watch out; otherwise I won't leave this apartment unfucked. And I know it won't be over with just a morning quickie. So, I lean forward to him and tease him with my breast floating above him, just as expected, his grip around my butt loosens as he tries to grab my breasts. I promptly seize the moment and slide off of him. Before he realizes what's happening, I get out of bed and dart a smug glance at him.

"I'm sorry, my dear, but I have to go to work," I purr, skillfully evading his arm that tries to pull me back.

"Now? To work? But it's only half past seven."

"Yes, but before that I have to go home and take a shower."

"You can also shower here," he says, watching me as I gather my clothes, leaning on his arm for support. "I promise you; I will wash you very thoroughly."

"Tempting offer. I'll consider it." And I mean it. Just the thought of Caleb and me in the shower... our naked, soapy bodies. His hands, exploring and caressing every inch of my body just like last night. A shiver of pleasure runs through me. I have to hold back from climbing into bed with him. "Now I need to get a taxi before I'm late." With these words, I pick up my black dress from the floor. When Caleb sees it, he sits up abruptly.

"Wait, you want to get into a taxi wearing that?" I look from my dress to Caleb.

"Of course, why not? I did the same last night."

"That's out of the question." In one fluid motion, he's on his feet, pulling out one of his Devil's sports suits from the closet. Then he takes me home on his racing bike. The ride is almost as sexy as our morning play. The motorcycle is designed in a way that I'm almost on him. My upper body and breasts are pressed firmly against his back, igniting my libido. I have no idea if he feels the same way, but it really gets me going. Just the scent of his leather jacket drives me wild. As he drops me off in front of our apartment building, I bid him farewell with a kiss infused with my desire. This forces a throaty groan from Caleb, pulling me closer to him. My lips are swollen when he finally releases me and swings back onto his bike. I look into his eyes, seeing raw desire shimmering within them, before he dons his helmet, the dark visor separating our gazes.

Then he starts his engine, letting it roar, and rides away. I stand by the road like an enamored teenager, watching him disappear. It's only when my phone, signaling its low battery, jolts me back to reality that I realize I should hurry. So, I rush up to our apartment, shower, and hastily get ready for work. Just as I'm searching for the car keys, I hear the apartment door. *Odd, Dad's first treatment isn't until eleven,* I think, making my way to the hallway. There, I spot my father, attempting to quietly lock the door. What's with all this secrecy?

"Dad?" I say, making him jump.

"Heavens, Emma, you startled me."

"What's going on with you? Where were you so early in the morning?" And then it hits me like a ton of bricks; he's just now coming home. Shit, now I notice how worn out he looks. His shirt is buttoned wrong, and his hair is tousled. And do I smell a woman's perfume on him? No, please, not this. A sharp pain shoots through my chest.

"Dad," I whisper, unbelievably taking a step back.

"I, well, I was with Bill. He and I..."

"Stop that, don't lie to me." He sighs and looks at me with exhaustion in his dull eyes. "You were with another woman; I can smell her perfume."

"Emma, I..."

"No, Dad. I don't want an apology. I want to finally know what's going on between Mom and you." Again, he sighs and pinches the bridge of his nose.

"Alright, but not here. Let's go to the kitchen, I need a

coffee." I nod, leading him through the hallway and sitting at one of the chairs at the dining table. From there, I watch as he fills the kettle and pours himself an instant coffee. In the meantime, Mom's sad face at Christmas haunts me. The call to Dad - he had his phone off. I remember being puzzled by it, since he's usually always reachable. Finally, my father joins me. He can't bring himself to look me in the eyes, keeping his gaze lowered to his coffee cup.

"Your mother and I have a few problems," he starts eventually. *Oh yes, you certainly do,* I think bitterly, *and I'm pretty sure I know what those problems are.* He runs his hand flat over his forehead. "I don't know how to say it..."

"Just say it straight. I'm a big girl and I'll handle it." *Handle the fact that you're cheating on Mom. Although I have to admit, I never would have thought it.* Another sigh and then the truth spills out of him.

"Your mother cheated on me with Marco, her tennis instructor. They've been having an affair for about ten months." My lips form a silent 'O'. I can't believe what he's saying.

"But Marco... He's your friend..."

"He was my tennis partner and friend for years, yes. Then your mother started taking tennis lessons from him and..." He trails off, rubbing the corners of his mouth. "You can imagine the rest." I can't believe it! She cheated on Dad, not the other way around! And then she has the audacity to sit in front of me with that mournful expression and whine. I just can't believe it.

"Your mother was my great love. When I found out what was going on between her and Marco, it broke my heart." The pain in my father's voice brings tears to my eyes. I want to get up and hug him, but I want him to finish his story. "I tried to forgive her. Believe me, I tried. But I couldn't. She left Marco, did everything to make it right again." He shakes his head, still looking down. "I didn't know what to do, only that I had to get out of Aberdeen. I couldn't bear the city with all the lies anymore. So, I called Bill." *His best friend from college,* I think, and I can understand him completely. If I had such a problem, Riley would be the first person I'd call too. "I was lucky; just two days before my call, the masseur of his team broke his arm and the Devils needed someone. It was like a fortunate twist of fate." I think of Caleb, wondering if it was destined for us to come here and meet him. If I'm honest, it feels that way. Even though the reason for us being here is terrible. "You know the rest of the story. I put my company on hold and moved to Portland with the most important thing left in my life: you."

"Oh, Dad!" I can't take it anymore, I jump out of my chair and throw my arms around him, crying. "I'm so terribly sorry." He says nothing, just raises a hand and holds me by the shoulder. I'm his anchor, all he has left, and I had no idea. "I'm here for you, Dad, always," I promise, sniffling. He nods and rubs his nose with his free hand. I force myself back into my chair but reach across the table and hold his hand tight. Finally, he looks up with reddened eyes. "Bill tried to cheer me up. He took me out and signed me up on a dating app. But it's not for me. I need to find myself again and process the separation from your mother before I dive into something new."

"And Mom? How is she dealing with all of this?"

Dad laughs bitterly. "She calls me incessantly, sends me texts, and begs me to come back. I had to turn off my phone because she was harassing me."

That's why he was unreachable during the holidays, and she was on the verge of tears. I'll have to talk to her, explain that there's no way back to Dad for her. Sometimes a relationship is irreversibly over. Maybe someone should explain that to that psycho girl Jessica.

"Your mother still holds on to the hope that I'll come back

to Aberdeen. But, Emma, that's the last thing I want. I'm done with this city and its people." Which ultimately means: We – meaning me, his anchor, and him – will never go back there. That's okay with me. I can still visit Mom and Riley on weekends if I feel like it. Besides, Portland offers more than one damn good reason to stay here forever.

We sit together at the table for a few more minutes before I reluctantly make my way to work. I arrive twenty minutes late to my massage room, where Parker is already waiting for his appointment. I claim to have overslept and am relieved that he doesn't hold my tardiness against me. As I warm up, the muscles of the winger for the weight room, the conversation with Dad goes through my head again. My heart is heavy with pity, and I decide to suggest to him that we start looking for a proper apartment. This two-room hole provided by the Devils shouldn't be more than a temporary solution. In a more spacious apartment, my father would surely feel more comfortable and at home. *Yes*, I think, *that's a good idea. I'll get a bunch of newspapers today and go through the ads.* After Parker, I have two more massages, which I use, among other things, to think about how we'll deal with Jessica. That issue is much trickier. Just as I'm setting up the table again, my phone chimes. I check and find a text from Caleb.

*You really should have climbed back into bed with me this morning. I miss you, almost forgot your taste. No idea how I'm going to make it through the day...'

Grinning, I reply:

*Maybe by looking forward to the evening already or...

I glance at the massage table behind me and write:

*... You come over and refresh your memory.

Caleb responds promptly:

*Fuck, Emma, you're driving me crazy!

This response makes me grin even wider. I can vivid-

Breaking the Ice

ly imagine Caleb adjusting his pants because they're getting tight. Then I receive another text from him.

*I'll take you up on your offer. But first, Parker and I have something to deal with. See you later.

This disappoints me now. I was in the mood for a bit of sexting. The thought of driving him crazy with a few dirty messages is damn tempting.

"Hey, kiddo," Dad stands in the doorway and looks at me. "I'm going to grab lunch. Do you want to join?" He looks better than he did this morning. That makes me happy.

"Sure, I'm in. How about Mexican?" I suggest, grabbing my handbag.

Lunch with Dad is great. We finally have some time to talk in peace. I tell him about my idea to get a bigger apartment. He's excited and wants to go through some listings with me later. Then I confess to him that he wasn't the only one who spent the night away. I believe we should be honest with each other. Surprisingly, he immediately figures out where I stayed. He noticed that Caleb has caught my eye; he knows me well. We don't mention Mom anymore. It's best not to poke at wounds that are in the process of healing. Before we head back to work, we agree to spend lunch together regularly. A bit of father-daughter time will be good for us.

Back at the ice rink, I finish my last massage for the day. Then I head home, freshen up, and pack some clothes because I assume I'll be staying with Caleb again tonight. This time, I want to savor the morning with him. While I tidy up the apartment a bit, I call Riley and tell her about Jessica and her threats. She's shocked and advises me not to take the situation lightly. She thinks someone crazy enough to bloody their own lips is capable of anything. Unfortunately, she can't think of a solution for our problem either. When I end the call, I'm just as clueless as before. Let's see, maybe Caleb has come up with something. I hope so!

I plan to head back to the ice rink at six to watch the guys' training. But just as I'm about to leave the apartment, Mom calls and wants to know where Dad is. Apparently, he's turned off his phone again. So, I sit down in the kitchen, make myself a tea, and talk to her. She's shocked when she finds out that I know about her affair. Of course, she immediately tries to explain her side of the story. She felt lonely because Dad was always working, and she longed for someone who loved her. A flimsy excuse, in my opinion. My father clearly loved her, or he wouldn't still be suffering like a dog today. In my eyes, Mom was simply bored with her housewife life and decided to have an affair. She's desperate because she lost him, but she brought this upon herself. I have to keep my composure and remind myself that she hasn't done anything to me. If the woman on the other end of the line wasn't my mother, I'd give her a piece of my mind without holding back. But in this situation, I force myself to stay calm. I advise her to leave Dad alone and explain that she will never have a chance with him again. She cries and tries over and over to convince me to talk to him on her behalf. But I stand firm. He's suffered enough, and I definitely won't put in a good word for her. When her tears finally stop, I encourage her, recommend meeting up with her girlfriends, and suggest finding a job to get back out in the world. That's all I can do for her at the moment – and all I want to do.

It's a quarter to eight when I finally manage to end the call. If it were up to Mom, we'd probably still be talking until tomorrow morning. But it's no use, I can't help her. She has to face this on her own."

On the way to the ice rink, I crank up my new favorite song, 'Call Out My Name' by The Weeknd, trying to shift my focus. My friend Mandy, who I've made plans with, is already waiting by the main entrance. Being the designated bet overseer's girlfriend, she has the privilege of joining in on this grand occasion. We hurry into the building and onto the ice, where most of the team has gathered. They are all in their Devils gear, complete with skates and the black training suits adorned with the red devil logo. As far as I know, it's Toby who has established the tradition of wearing these suits for bet settlements. Caleb and I notice each other at the same time. I can see the tension around his mouth fade away, replaced by a smile that makes my heart flutter. *Wow, it's only now that I realize how much I'd missed him in those few hours.*

"You were gone for quite a while," he remarks as he passes through the heavy door to join me on the player's bench. Then he pulls me close and kisses me with a passion that sent shivers down to my core. I can't help but moan into his mouth, my hands finding their way into his locks. In an instant, all the desire that had been simmering within me throughout the day surges back.

"Hey, you two, either get a room or compose yourselves!" Toby interrupts us, arriving with Durand and Parker in tow. I turn to them and burst into laughter. Their penalty attire consists of nothing more than skates and black boxers. Well, at least that's the case for Durand, because Parker is sporting an additional helmet and a comically looking protective cup over his shorts. With his slender frame, he looks like an oversized pin or a worm with a helmet. It is hilariously absurd. While the two of them skate past us onto the ice, Toby turns to his girlfriend. He greets her with a kiss and takes the golden hockey stick she has brought for him. Then he comes over to us, giving me a wink and patting Caleb on the shoulder.

"Come on, let's get this started," he says, rushing out onto the ice.

Breaking the Ice

"See you in a bit," my forward murmurs, stealing one more kiss before following the Swiss player. As the team forms a half-circle around Toby, Durand, and Parker, I sit down next to Mandy on the bench. We watch with bated breath as the lights dim and a spotlight focuses on the goalie.

"Dear betting enthusiasts, we have gathered here today to witness Ethan Parker and Pascal Durand settle their debt!" Two more spotlights illuminate the two underwear-clad players.

"These two gentlemen believed they could conquer our resilient masseuse, Emma, and they failed miserably!" Toby dramatically points with the end of his golden stick at the losers. "And now..."

He raises a small, shiny object. "I shall determine who goes first using this coin."

"Isn't he incredible?" gushes my friend beside me. I have to admit, Toby is doing an excellent job as the bet overseer. We watch as he negotiates with Parker and Durand to decide who calls heads and who calls tails. Then he flicks the coin, catches it, and claps it onto the back of his hand.

"Tails! Parker goes first!" The players cheer and Parker skates up to the upper half of the rink, positioning himself on a red X spray-painted onto the ice.

"I can't even watch," Mandy whines. "Can you imagine how much a puck must hurt?"

"No, but I can only assume it's excruciatingly painful."

"Parker is seriously stupid for participating in something like this. He's got no one to blame but himself if he ends up like Toby."

"Why, what happened to Toby?"

"Don't you know the story of how he got his Big Ben?" I know many stories about Toby, but not this one.

"I'm telling you, the guy's a complete idiot. Back when he

played for London, he lost a bet, same stakes as Parker. The only difference was, he had to step onto the ice stark naked, no cup, no helmet. And guess what? He took a puck right to the family jewels."

"Damn! That sounds brutal."

"Yep. Ever since, he's been down to one bell - his 'Big Ben', as they call it." It's not exactly a laughing matter, but I can't help but crack a smile.

"Once our audience is ready, we can continue!" Toby calls out to us.

"We're all set, babe! Let's get this show on the road!" Mandy signals to her beau. I steal a glance at Caleb. He's got his sights on Parker. I watch as Durand takes his position on a second red X, about 15 meters in front of the first. Toby, riding alongside him, raises a puck into the air.

"Parker's punishment is three shots!" he announces, handing Durand three of the rubber pucks and the golden stick. Then he looks towards the tech room. "Larry, let's go!" *Larry, the janitor?* In the next moment, a drumroll echoes through the hall. *I have to admit, the guys have put some effort into this.* Durand raises his stick and winds up as the drum roll crescendos. Then he strikes, with Larry adding a drumbeat for effect. He hits Parker on the shoulder. Parker jerks in pain.

"Fuck! You jerk!" he bellows, rubbing the red spot. Durand's second shot ricochets off Parker's helmet. If Parker wasn't wearing one, he'd probably be in the market for a new set of teeth. The third and final shot is the worst. It connects with Parker's thigh, clearly injuring him. Mandy and I jump up, alarmed to see blood trickling down his leg.

"It's okay, don't worry, just a little cut!" Toby reassures us. *Just a little cut? Let's hope he's right...* "Ladies and gentlemen, I ask for a round of applause for Ethan Parker, who has settled his debt here!" The players clap, Parker rejoins the others, and

Breaking the Ice

Durand... He tosses his stick aside and makes a dash for the open door in front of us. *He's trying to escape!*

"Durand!" Toby's voice reverberates through the hall. "Don't you dare!" The Canadian stops right before the exit. His feverish gaze tells me he's weighing whether to stay or bolt. Too late, Toby catches up to him. "I'm warning you; you won't make it as far as you can piss until I drag you back by the balls," the goalie growls. "A bet's a bet. That goes for maggots like you too. Now get back here." He nudges him towards the team. Surprisingly, Durand gives in and returns.

"Let's carry on. Byers!" The defenseman approaches Toby, who has resumed his original spot between Parker and Durand. He hands Byers a red velvet cushion, on which rests an electric hair trimmer. "Now, onto Durand's bet: a bald head and shaved eyebrows! Parker!" He hands the giant pin the trimmer, steps aside, and gives a clear view. Mandy and I watch in fascination as Parker revs up the machine and places it against Durand's forehead. Durand tenses up and clenches his fists in desperation. Then the steady hum transitions into a duller noise, and Durand's flow is parted right down the middle. We watch, jaws dropping, as Parker systematically strips away the Canadian's dark locks, leaving him with nothing but mousey eyes. And a - as I notice for the first time - pretty crooked nose. No amount of muscles or tattoos can compensate for that. As soon as the duo exits the stage, the others leave the ice as well.

"What a show!" Mandy praises as her sweetheart, and Caleb, join us on the player's bench.

"Yeah, right? Those two really pulled it off," he replies with a grin. "What's next? Shall we grab a drink together?"

"Sorry, buddy, not tonight," Caleb answers. When I step up beside him, he wraps an arm around me.

"I understand," Toby says, grinning broadly. He knows we have other plans. "That's fine. Baby, more time for us then."

He wiggles his blond brows and playfully swats his girlfriend's backside before they head off, leaving Caleb to look down at me.

"So, what do you say we head to my place?" His voice carries a dark undertone.

"Absolutely. I just need to grab something from the massage room real quick." An enticing idea occurred to me earlier today, involving lots of warm oil and our naked bodies.

"Sounds good. I'll just change my shoes real quick." He gestures to his training bag at the end of the player's bench.

"See you in a bit." I rise on my tiptoes to give him a kiss and hurry downstairs to my massage room. Once there, I search the shelf for a suitable oil and find a natural almond oil. Perfect! Just as I'm about to grab the bottle, I sense I'm no longer alone. I turn around and see Caleb leaning in the doorway, arms crossed. He gives me a look that shoots straight between my legs. Suddenly, he pushes off and comes to me. Then he lifts me into his arms, heads back to the door, closes it, and locks it.

20

CALEB

"What's this? Is someone feeling impatient?" Emma teases, as I carry her to the table and gently lower her onto it. I don't answer, instead, I step between her legs and pull her shirt over her head. As my hands trace down her back to reach for the bra clasp, I lower my head and kiss her. Her taste feels like a firework in my mouth and makes my cock throb.

All day long I've been walking around with a hard on. One thought of Emma was enough to make it erect. Now I can't and will not wait any longer. Her bra slides down her body and lands on the floor. My hands glide towards her breasts and pluck on her already hard nipples. This triggers a soft moan from my beauty. She lets go of me and directs her gaze at the door. She is worried someone could come and interrupt us. *I will let you forget about everything but us*, I think.

I unbutton her jeans. "Lift your ass," I command and pull it off including the panties and her pumps. Then I kneel down, dive between her thighs and slide my tongue across her already wet hole. *Fuck, I love her juice!* I take care of Emma's puffy pussy, indulge in her clitoris and make her pant heavily in minutes. Her hands run through my curls, pull eagerly on my hair while I drive her closer. But I don't have the intention to make her come like this. I rise and kiss her neck. Emma's finger finds the zipper under my training jacket, open it and pull it from my shoulders. The next moment I feel her hands wander over my chest down to my waistband. Quickly I pull out a condom from my pants before my training shorts slide down to my ankles. I straighten up and see the desire in her eyes as she licks across her hand and reaches for my cock. I inhale sharply through my teeth. Her touch almost makes my dick explode. She plays with it, pushes me equally as fast as I pushed her. Then she takes the oil besides us, presses the bottleneck against my collarbone and lets the liquid drip down on me. With her free hand she spreads the marzipan smelling oil on my upper body. Meanwhile I put on the condom. I reach for her thigh, pull her to the edge of the massage table and with a single thrust I bury my cock inside her.

"Yes, Caleb!" she moans. Her hands on my neck, she lowers her gaze on my stiffy. She watches as I pump into her with increasing frequency, *Holy shit, this girl is definitely not uptight.* She enjoys watching as I fuck her. This realization makes me even harder. After a few more thrusts, she pushes me away and jumps from the massage table.

"What's the matter?" I ask perplexed. But Emma just gives me a seductive smile, jumps in her pumps and turns around to present me her backside. Then she hands me the oil and leans with her arms on the massage table. Now I have her wonderful butt in front of me.

I immediately understand what she wants, open the bottle, and soak the rose on her lower back with oil. I draw a trail downward, stopping only when the oil reaches her ass cheeks. Then I hand her the bottle back and spread the liquid on her ass. A stunning view, her skin, the tribal tattoo with the rose, the dreamcatcher on her left cheek, all covered by a shiny thin film. I can't hold back any longer, I thrust in her tight pussy while I grab her tighter by the hips with every following push. This position must drive her wild since she immediately starts breathing heavier. I caress her butt, spread it a bit so I can see her anus. Fuck, I can't help it, I have to touch it. Then I push the tip of my finger in. This finishes Emma off. "God, yes!" I feel her pussy gripping tighter and her muscles clenching as she comes. Carefully I pull my finger out of her. Just as I try to grab her hips to finish myself, she escapes my grip a second time.

"Emma...?"

"Shh." With a lever she lowers the massage table before she sits on it, gesturing with her index finger for me to come closer. I step between her spread legs while she once again puts oil on her hands, removes the condom and rubs it on my dick. I blink down at her in confusion as she caresses the tip of my cock around her pierced nipple. I suddenly I understand: She lets me come on her. *Holy shit, how hot is she?* My cock twitches eagerly in her hand. With a naughty smile, she begins to rub from tip to shaft. It takes less than two minutes, until my balls start to tingle, and I come all over her breasts. "Fuck Emma," I moan as I grab her chin to lift it for a kiss. Her taste makes me twitch one last time in her hand. My forehead pressed against hers, I take a deep breath. I think I might have heard something in the hallway, and hurry with cleaning Emma up with some towels from the bathroom. Then we dress up, wipe of the spilled oil and change the cover of the massage table before we leave.

Upon arriving in my loft, we shower together and order a pizza. We devour it on the couch, which we subsequently grace with our body fluids. It's past midnight when we finally lie in my bed.

"Caleb?" Emma asks sleepily.

"Hmm?"

"Do you already know what you want to do about Jessica?"

"Yes, I called her and asked her to come here tomorrow afternoon." Immediately, she tenses up. She doesn't like the idea of my ex coming to my place, and I understand that. But there's no way I'm going to her, dealing with her mother. She never had a kind word for me, even before we broke up. She'd interfere, and her snake tongue is the last thing I need. I absolutely need to meet Jess somewhere where she can speak openly. "It's the only way," I explain. "I have to reason with her, and I can only do that in a one-on-one conversation."

"And what if she won't listen? Then you'll choose her over me."

"No. Never."

"You'll have to, because otherwise she'll ruin your career. And that can't happen."

"I'll find a way, I promise." Emma lifts her head and looks at me sadly. Her gaze shifts between my eyes. "I don't want to lose you, Caleb." Her words cut through my chest, deeper than any 'I love you' I've ever heard.

"You won't. I won't allow it," I reply, lifting her chin with my index finger and kissing her.

It will be one of the shortest nights of my life. I lie awake for ages, looking at Emma and contemplating what exactly I should say to Jess.

The mood the next morning is melancholic. Emma and I hardly talk, but we hold and kiss each other all the more passionately. When I drop her off at the ice rink, I have this disgusting feeling like I might have to say goodbye to her forever. It's hard for me to let her go, I pull her back to me by the motorcycle over and over, kissing her. Eventually, she has to go because Toby is waiting for his massage. I watch her until she disappears into the building. Then I start my engine and

Breaking the Ice

ride off. I have a few things to take care of before Jess arrives.

One minute before four, the doorbell rings at my apartment. My stomach is a fiery lump as I open the door for my ex-girlfriend and invite her in. *This has to work out!* Jessica is dressed up, wearing her little black dress, and the air is tainted with an overpowering perfume.

"Can I offer you something to drink?" I ask, leading her to the poker table where I offer her a chair.

"Has this table always been here in the middle of the room?" she asks, surprised, and takes a seat.

"Yes," I lie, redirecting her attention back to my original question. "Water, coffee? What would you like?"

Jess runs her tongue over her lips and grins. Me. Why do I bother asking? I drop the drink question, take a chair, and sit diagonally across from her at the table.

"So, Caleb, you said you wanted to talk?" I hate the smug smile she wears when she says these words. "I assume you've reconsidered my demand. Spit it out, how have you decided?"

"You mean, you want to know who you get to torment. Me, by hurting yourself and claiming I did it, or Emma, by doing... what? Asking your daddy to fire her? That alone won't be enough. Because you know what, Emma not only excels at her job, but she's also the team's favorite."

I cross my legs and fold my fingertips together. "You have nothing against her."

"Caleb..." Jess smirks. "... Do you really think I'm that naive? Of course, I have something against your slit-eyed girl." *Don't call her that, you piece of garbage!* screams the voice in my head. Still, I force myself to stay calm and not let my anger show.

"And what would that be?"

"You'll find out soon enough. Now, tell me your decision."

"You know, I just can't wrap my head around why you're

doing this. I mean, all doors are open to you in life. Why waste your time with Emma and me?"

"Because you betrayed me, and that bitch took you away from me. She's taken possession of what's rightfully mine."

"And that's reason enough for you to destroy our lives?"

"Absolutely. You should've thought about whether you wanted to cross me before."

It's clear, she won't be reasoned with, I realize. Tense, I run my hand flatly over my mouth. One last attempt.

"Alright, how much do you want?"

"Money?" She raises an amused eyebrow. "Caleb, my family is swimming in money. Do you seriously think I need your dough? Don't make a fool of yourself."

I grit my teeth. "Alright, then tell me what you want. Tell me what I can do to make you leave us alone," I press, put my legs together, and lean forward on my elbows.

"Oh, there's actually something. Dump the slut and come back to me. Maybe then I'll reconsider whether or not to fire her."

"That's out of the question!"

"Well, then," she says sharply, "I suggest you make a decision quickly. You have until tomorrow evening at ten o'clock." She gets up and looks down at me coldly. "Don't even think I'm bluffing. I have nothing to lose. Decide against your little girlfriend, or I'll make sure my father makes your life a living hell and ends your career."

I knew she would say that; I don't need to hear more. Now I get up too.

"Leave, now!" My harsh tone doesn't surprise her. On the contrary, she shrugs her slender shoulders and totters to the door. Once there, she sighs and turns to me one last time.

"You know, Caleb, you really should seriously consider whether you want to jeopardize your future for some girl. Just think how hard your way into the pro league was. There isn't a pussy in the world who is worth risking your career for." With that, she grabs the doorknob and disappears for good.

21

EMMA

After Caleb drops me off at the ice rink, the uneasy feeling that has been bothering me since early this morning intensifies. I'm shaky and my hands are cold. All morning, I feel out of sorts. God, I fervently hope that Jessica will be willing to talk. I can't eat anything during the lunch break, which worries Dad. I tell him I'm not feeling well, which isn't even a lie, as my stomach feels far from healthy. Shortly after half past three, my last massage for today comes to an end. Now, a terrible tension overwhelms me, knowing that Caleb will soon meet with Jessica. To distract myself, I go shopping. Caleb and I have plans to meet at my place at eight tonight. I want to officially introduce him to Dad as my new boyfriend over dinner. As I wander through the aisles of the supermarket, gathering all the ingredients for lasagna, I keep glancing at my phone. No messages, no calls. It's driving me crazy! When I get home, I put away the groceries and send Dad a text reminding him of dinner at eight. It's half past four now. Are they still talking? I decide to distract myself with housework. After all, I want everything to be neat when Caleb comes over tonight. An hour later, I can't take it anymore and I text him.

Everything okay with you? How did the conversation with Jessica go?

With a pounding heart, I wait for a reply. But it doesn't come. I tell myself he's probably at practice and hasn't seen my message yet. Then I start making the lasagna so it'll be ready on time.

Seven minutes past eight, my dad arrives. "Sorry, I'm late! Bill talked me into having a beer after practice!" he calls from the hallway. "Mmm, that already smells delicious," he praises and comes into the kitchen to me. When he sees me sitting at the set table, arms wrapped around my stomach, aching with worry, he stops abruptly.

"Emma? What's wrong, what's going on? And where's Caleb?"

"He's not here."

"I can see that. But why? I was sure he'd be here by now. He even skipped practice. I thought you'd be cooking together."

"He skipped practice?" Has something happened to him? Suddenly I panic, thinking Jessica might have done something to him. It wouldn't be beyond that crazy woman.

"Yeah, Bill's pretty mad about it. The guys have their first playoff game coming up. Training sessions are crucial."

That's true, and it's so unlike Caleb to miss training. I'm about to get up to go look for him when my phone, sitting next to me on the table, beeps. With a dreadful feeling, I pick it up and see that I've received a text. It's from Caleb.

Have to cancel dinner, something's come up.

A fiery pain shoots through my stomach as I realize: I've

worried for nothing. He's fine, he just doesn't want to see me. With tears in my eyes, I stare at the screen. Meanwhile, Dad grabs a chair and sits directly in front of me.

"Emma, I want to know what's going on now. Please, sweetheart, talk to me." I swallow the painful lump in my throat and lift my gaze. A single tear rolls down my cheek as I look into Dad's warm eyes.

"Let me be your anchor, just like you are mine," he says softly, placing his hand on my knee. And with that, the dam breaks. I nod and tearfully tell him about Caleb and me. How we got together and how he means more to me than anyone before. I also tell him about Jessica, her demand, and how Caleb tried to talk to her again today. He listens attentively, furrowing his brow when I show him the text where Caleb cancels our dinner.

I pour out all my heartache. Finally, I let Dad hold me in his arms and comfort me. Then he serves himself a plate of lasagna and we go to the living room. While he settles into his chair, I lie down on the couch. I have a terrible headache. My father reassures me, saying I have to wait and see what tomorrow brings. Maybe everything will turn out for the better. In his eyes, Jessica is nothing more than a spoiled brat used to getting what she wants. He believes Mr. Flake is sensible enough not to fire me just because his girl demands it. His deep voice is soothing to me. Eventually, I grow sleepy, so Dad gets my bedding and tucks me in. I know him, he'll sit up late in front of the TV, keeping watch over me. That's why I love him. He's there for me when I'm feeling down.

"Sleep well, my darling," he whispers, brushing the back of his hand against my cheek.

"Dad?" I say with heavy eyelids.

"Hm?"

"It looks like we've both been betrayed, doesn't it?"

"Let's hope not," he replies solemnly. "Now sleep, I'm here." He gives me his everything-will-be-alright smile and settles back into his chair. Then he quietly turns on the TV and starts eating his now-cold lasagna.

The next morning, he wakes me up at eight o'clock. I immediately check my phone, but to my disappointment, there's neither a text nor a call from Caleb. Unable to bear the uncertainty any longer, I call him, but he doesn't pick up. I leave him a voicemail, asking him to call me back. Then I get ready for work. Dad forces me to eat something before we head to the ice rink. Arriving there, I feel desolate and empty, much like the gloomy gray sky over Portland. Alongside my father, I descend the stairs to our massage rooms.

"Don't freak out, Emma," he pleads as we walk down the hallway and turn the corner. "You'll see..." He stops abruptly and stands still when he spots Jessica and Mr. Flake in front of my massage room.

"No," I whisper, feeling something inside me break. *That's it, it's official now. Caleb has chosen against me and for his career. I know I suggested it to him myself. But secretly, I had hoped he wouldn't go through with it.* I see Dad shoot me a pained look. His expression says it all: *You were right, my dear, it looks like we've both been betrayed.* Then he clears his throat, squares his shoulders, and approaches the two of them. He will advocate for me, protect me. I swallow down the pain. Now you have to be brave, I tell myself, straightening my own shoulders and following my father.

"Mr. Flake, what brings us the honor?"

When the man in the wheelchair spots us, his face darkens.

"I'm not here because of you, Maxwell, but because of your daughter," he barks, passing by Dad and heading straight for me. "You!" His finger points accusingly at me while Jessica

Breaking the Ice

grins maliciously behind him. "How dare you try to poison my boys with this garbage?" He tosses a small plastic bag to me, which I reflexively catch. It's transparent and filled with yellow pills, on which a smiley face can be seen. I look at the pills with furrowed brows, realizing what Jessica's plan is.

"Did you think I wouldn't find out, or what? You're fired! On the spot!"

"Just a moment! What is this about? What are you accusing my daughter of?" Dad intervenes and comes over to us. Behind him, Jessica slithers towards me like a snake.

"Your daughter tried to sell drugs to my players. Jessica saw with her own eyes how she tried to sell these pills to Durand."

"That can't be true, she would never do something like that."

"Oh, so you're claiming my daughter is lying?"

"I'm saying that Emma is a decent girl and has nothing to do with drugs."

"Well, if your child is as decent as you claim, then please explain to me how we found these pills on her!" Mr. Flake gets louder with every word. His head is as red as a tomato. "If there's one thing I strictly forbid my team, it's drugs. And then your daughter comes along, trying to peddle her crap to the boys!" Still holding the plastic bag, I helplessly look back and forth between the two men.

"I told you already, Emma doesn't deal! Where did this trash even come from? Who says it's hers?"

"We searched her massage room and found the pills hidden under the cushion of the table! So, what do you say now? Are you still convinced your sunshine is innocent?!"

"Then someone must have planted it on her."

"Please, Maxwell, don't make a fool of yourself."

"What do you think, Emma?" Jessica hisses quietly, stepping closer to me as our fathers debate fervently. "Didn't I

Breaking the Ice

find a good hiding spot under the freshly covered table where you and Caleb had your fun last night?" What? I look at her in disbelief. Caleb was right, someone was outside the door!

"Don't look so dumbstruck; I heard you two. You had a lot of fun. But where is he now, your great lover?" She raises her hands and looks around in an exaggerated manner. "Looks like he's leaving you in the lurch." Jessica feigns a sympathetic expression. "Well, it seems you've lost. Caleb has left you." Hearing these words from her mouth is like receiving a slap in the face. I don't know if I'd rather wipe the smug grin off her face or just run away.

"You can twist and turn it all you want, Emma brought drugs into my ice rink. That's why she's fired!" I hear Mr. Flake say coldly next to us. I turn my attention to my father, who places his hands on his hips.

"If you fire my daughter, I'll leave too."

"Please, feel free. You're not the only sports masseurs in this world. Bill will find a replacement." Mr. Flake's mouth is pressed into a misshapen scar as he looks from my father to me. "You pack your things and get out. Today!" he growls, passing me by. I know he won't believe my words any more than he believes my father's. Still, I have to try. Even though Caleb has left me, I don't want to leave Portland and lose Toby and the others.

"Sir, please, I know it looks like the pills belong to me. But I really have nothing to do with them."

"Save your breath, girl. It's over." I'm about to explain to him that his daughter set this up when I hear footsteps. Many footsteps! The four of us look down the hallway, where Toby and the other players come around the corner. I spot Byers, Parker, and even the eyebrow-less Durand, who's wearing a Devils cap and looks like he'd rather be anywhere else. Only Caleb isn't with them. The guys head straight towards us and

Breaking the Ice

stop just in front of the wheelchair.

"What are you doing here?" Flake wants to know.

"Preventing you from making a mistake," Toby explains, briefly glancing over at me, as if to make sure I'm okay, then turning back to his boss. "Is it true? Did you fire Emma?" *How does he know?*

"That's none of your business, now let me through." Flake tries to squeeze past Toby and Byers, but the guys form a human wall with their bodies.

"No, we won't." Toby's water-blue eyes remain unwaveringly fixed on the owner. *They're all here because of me,* I realize, and I'm so touched that I could cry. At least I mean something to them.

"Emma is our good luck charm!" one of the guys from the back calls out.

"Yes, you can't possibly fire her. Especially now when the playoffs are starting. We need her," Byers adds.

"Well, if your charm is so valuable, then you'll have to find another one," Flake responds sternly. "I won't tolerate drug dealers under my roof."

"If that's the case, you'll have to look for a new winger," a voice interjects, sending shivers down my spine. My heart catches fire. Can it really be? Is he here? I watch as the rows of players part to let Caleb through. Indeed, he's come. I can hardly believe it. Does that mean he didn't actually leave me? I would love to run to him and throw myself into his arms. But I hold back. His gaze briefly meets mine before it travels down to the plastic bag in my hand.

"What do you mean I need a new winger? What are you trying to tell me, Caleb?"

"Your anger is directed at the wrong person. This stuff..." He gestures at the drugs in my hand. "...Belongs to Durand, and none other than your daughter planted it on Emma."

Breaking the Ice

"What a lie!" Jessica exclaims with a shrill voice.

"How dare you accuse Jessica!"

"Please, Carl." Caleb's hand rests on Mr. Flake's shoulder. "Give me five minutes to explain what's going on here." Flake's face is contorted with anger, but he remains silent, prompting Caleb to continue. "Durand uses these pills to make women compliant." He turns to his teammates. "Do you remember Emma's first night at Brillant? Do you recall how dazed she seemed towards the end? He slipped half a pill into her Long Island."

"You did what?" I exclaim, staring at the Canadian in disbelief. So, that's why I felt so awful.

"You're a dead man," Toby growls, grabbing him by the collar.

"Damn it, this is all your fault, Jess!" Durand shouts. "You said nothing could go wrong." Now, all eyes turn to the blonde.

"I have no idea what you're talking about!"

"You know exactly. You begged me to give you the pills so you could get back at Caleb."

"What? You're lying! You've all conspired against me!" The beast turns to her father's side, seeking refuge. "Daddy, you have to believe me. I have nothing to do with these drugs!"

"Just like you had nothing to do with trying to blackmail me? Demanding that I choose between my career and Emma?" Caleb asks.

"I have no idea what you're talking about. I don't need to blackmail anyone."

"Oh really? Parker?" Caleb turns to his buddy, who nods and steps out from the crowd.

"Mr. Flake, if you would please take a look at this. I recorded it yesterday afternoon in Caleb's loft." Parker taps on his phone and hands it over to his boss. Flake takes the smartphone with a furrowed brow and looks down at the display.

Breaking the Ice

Everyone present listens eagerly.

"So, Caleb, you said you wanted to talk? I assume you've reconsidered my demand. Spit it out, how have you decided?" Jessica's voice emanates from the speaker. Dad and I approach Flake from behind and glance over his shoulder at the phone in his hand. On the display, we see Caleb and his ex, sitting at his poker table, talking. Judging by the angle, the video was taken from the stairs leading to his bedroom.

"No, Daddy, don't watch this!" Jessica exclaims. She reaches down, attempting to snatch the device from her father's hand, but he catches her arm and pushes her aside.

"Shhh, I want to see it." Now it's her turn to look dumbfounded. I refrain from making a snarky comment and instead watch the video. Caleb is brilliant. He skillfully guides the conversation so that she gradually spills the beans. I see Mr. Flake tensing up as he realizes what a deceitful person his daughter is. He watches the entire video before looking up at his forward with remorse.

"Do you believe me now, Carl? Emma has nothing to do with these drugs." Caleb steps to my side and takes the plastic bag from my hand. His fingers graze my skin tenderly, sending shivers down my spine. He smiles at me and then turns back to the boss. "These," he explains, handing him the pills, "belong to Durand, not Emma. I know he has more stashed in his locker."

"Sir, please, I never took any of these myself, nor did I sell them to any of the guys. You have to believe me," Durand pleads. He's still hanging from Toby's grip, looking utterly desperate.

"To my office," says the owner.

"Sir, please!"

"Immediately!" Flake thunders, turning to the other players. "All of you, take this as a lesson. I won't tolerate drugs

Breaking the Ice

in my team. Now, get out, I have work to do." He presses a button on the armrest of his wheelchair, causing it to make a tight turn and stop in front of Jessica. She backs away like a trapped animal.

"And now, you. I am profoundly disappointed. You'll never set foot in my ice rink again, I can tell you that much. We'll sort out the rest later. Go home, I'll deal with you later." As the blonde girl stomps past her old man, teeth gritted and face crimson, he turns to Dad and me.

"I have to apologize to both of you. I had no way of knowing what intrigues were being spun behind the scenes. If you still want to, Emma, you can keep your job." I'm still so overwhelmed by everything that just happened that I can only nod in silence.

"Very well, then welcome back, good luck charm," he says contentedly, then turns around and follows the guys.

"I'll leave you two alone," Dad smiles at me, kisses my forehead, and leaves. I blink up at Caleb, who steps in front of me, looking down at me with a serious expression.

"I'm sorry," he says softly, taking my hands in his. His touch tightens my throat. God, how I've missed being close to him. "I didn't want to leave you thinking I had chosen against you, but I had to. It was the only chance to get both Jessica and Durand."

"I don't understand…" My voice is rough, like sandpaper.

"I didn't tell you about my plan because Jessica could never see that we were trying to fool her. She had to take the bait and believe that I had chosen against you. That was the only way to make sure she stayed here, and I could expose her in front of everyone."

"You planned all of this?"

"Yes. After Parker made that video yesterday afternoon, I waited for two hours and then called Jess. I told her I had reconsidered her words and had chosen my career. Then I got her to reveal her plan. I made her believe I wanted to avoid running into you again, so I needed to know when exactly she was going to expose you. She was so confident that she had won that she just told me everything. About the drugs, where she had hidden them, and when she was planning to blow your cover." Unbelievable – and I was so sure he had chosen against me. I feel the painful weight that has been on my chest since last night start to lift.

"I thought you left me," I whisper, looking between his wonderful eyes.

"Emma," Caleb says gently, cupping my face in his hands. His thumb catches the single tear rolling down my cheek. "I would never leave you. Not for my career or anything else in this world." He leans down so I can feel his breath tingling on my skin. "You belong to me," he murmurs, "and no one will ever take you away from me." With that, he lowers his lips to mine and seals his words with a long, intense kiss.

Epilogue

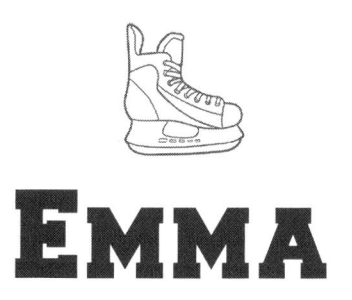

Emma

Ten days later.

Lost in thought, I stand at the foot of my bed, absentmindedly fiddling with the button on the quilt. Today, the Devils had their first playoff game, which they managed to win with a score of three to two. It was an insane match. Caleb and his guys were unbelievably good, and even Durand gave it his all. That says something, considering he's been through a pretty rough time. After Mr. Flake found out about the drugs, he really grilled him. Durand didn't get kicked out, but he had to undergo a drug test - which came back negative. Plus, Flake insisted he turns himself in for slipping those pills to me and the other girls. I know the Canadian contemplated leaving the team amidst all this trouble. It was Caleb himself who took care of his teammate. He believes that every person in this world deserves a second chance. Even Durand. Although he still harbors resentment for him, for slipping me that half tablet back then. Anyway, Caleb persuaded him to stay, not to hang up his career and waste his talent. Thanks to him, the winger has pulled himself together again. A lot has changed otherwise. We haven't seen Jessica up to this day; according to Bill, her father forbade her from contacting his players for life. He was horrified that his daughter was the one sabotaging his team. Dad and Mom had a two-hour conversation. She apologized for abusing his trust, and finally realized she couldn't make amends. They filed for divorce. It pains me to see them suffer, but I know it's the only right thing to do.

"But you do realize you're occupying the bed for free, don't you?" I glance over my shoulder and spot Caleb strolling into my new bedroom and towards me. Dad and I found this wonderful four-room apartment very close to the ice rink.

"I had originally planned for us to spend the night here," I respond, sensing a subtle twinge in my lower abdomen. Caleb and I have only ever stayed at his loft, for the simple reason that we can't seem to keep our hands off each other. At his place, we can be as loud as we want, and we don't have to worry about my dad overhearing. I had actually planned to stay here tonight. But the way Caleb is looking at me right now, it's going to be tough to stick to my plan. He embraces me from behind and pulls me close.

"We can do that tomorrow... or the day after," he whispers into my ear with a seductive voice. I feel his breath tickling my neck before he kisses the curve of it. His tongue traces a moist trail up to my earlobe, sending shivers down my spine. Caleb grins against my neck. He knows exactly how I respond to his proximity, and he revels in it.

"Just you wait!" I let go of the bedding and turn to face him. It's incredible, I love that hungry look in his eyes.

I raise my arms, entwining my hands around his neck, and press myself closer to him. Judging by the corner of his mouth twitching, he can feel my hard nipples through the thin fabric of my cocktail dress. "You know," I purr, rising up on my tiptoes to playfully nip at his lower lip, "I'd much rather strip you down right here and now, push you onto my bed, and pick up where we left off this morning." Caleb's eyes darken. "Is that so?" There is a hint of excitement in his voice.

"Yes, I would soil this bed with every trick in the book, suck your dick, let it slide deep down my throat..."

"And now," I whisper, suppressing a grin, "we have to go, or we'll be late for the party at Brillant." With that, I quickly slip out of his grip and step past him to the door.

"Hey, how are you two doing?" Dad appears in the open doorway.

"Good," I reply, giving Caleb a smirk. He squints at me with a "just you wait" look. The doorbell rings.

"That must be Bill," my father guesses, leading the way. I'm about to follow him when Caleb takes my hand and pulls me back towards him. I laugh, thinking he's teasing or trying to be playful. But his expression is surprisingly serious. With furrowed brows, I look up at him. He lifts a hand and gently tucks a strand of hair behind my ear. His gaze follows his fingers as they trace along my jawline and to my cheek.

"Thank you," he says earnestly, then fixes his wonderful brown eyes on mine.

"For what?" I ask, nestling my face into his warm palm.

"For giving us both a chance." A brief but sharp pain shoots through my stomach as I remember the evening outside the cigar shop. Back then, a future together with him seemed unimaginable to me. Yet we've managed to make it, forging our path despite all odds. "A life without you is unthinkable for me." Caleb's voice is soft but fervent. It pierces deep into my chest, making me realize that I feel more for this man than I ever have for anyone else. His hands cradle my face as our gazes meld together. "I love you, Emma," he says, filling my heart with overflowing happiness.

Breaking the Ice

"I love you too," I reply, my voice choked with emotion. The smile he gives me makes my knees go weak. He leans down and kisses me. As the world around us fades into oblivion, and I'm aware only of his presence, one thought pierces through:

My new job here was more than just a stroke of luck. It was fate because Caleb and I are meant for each other.

The End.

About the Author

Christine Troy was born in 1981 in Dornbirn, Austria. Happily married, she still resides in the picturesque Vorarlberg with her husband and their two children. She only discovered her passion for writing in her late twenties. In 2015, she transitioned from writing young adult fantasy to romance, where she has gained a large and steadily growing fanbase. Alongside writing, Christine works as a voice-over artist.

Our books are also available in e-book. Find our catalog on:
https://cherry-publishing.com/en/

Subscribe to our newsletter and receive a free e-book! You'll also receive the latest updates on all of our upcoming publications!

https://mailchi.mp/b78947827e5e/get-your-free-ebook

Editorial manager: Audrey Puech
Composition and layout: Cherry Publishing
Interior Illustrations: © Shutterstock
Cover design: Keti Matakov
Cover illustration: Keti Matakov